When Bad Things Happen To Good People

God Explains Life's Mysteries, Problems and Wisdom

Merton Lee

Dedicated to Dr Billy Graham, Dr Charles Stanley,
Dr Charles Swindoll, Dr Rick Warren,
Brother David Steindl-Rast, Ms Elisabeth Elliot,
Ms Oprah Winfrey, Ms Joni Eareckson Tada,
Mr Harold Kushner, Mr Philip Yancey,
Mr Don Piper, Professor Eugene Peterson,
Thich Nhat Hanh, Dr Roger Walsh, Ram Dass,
Dr Jack Kornfield, Ms Sharon Salzberg,
Ms Sylvia Boorstein, Dr Wayne Dyer,
Ms Louise Hay, Mr Eckhart Tolle and Mr Gary Zukav
for their warmth, love and encouragement
which they keep bringing to us
in the different seasons of life.

Contents

A Spring of Hope
(Sharing His Messages of Hope, Love and Truth)

A Light exists in Spring
Not present on the Year
At any other period.
When March is scarcely here

A Color stands abroad
On Solitary Fields
That Science cannot overtake,
But Human Nature feels.

It waits upon the Lawn,
It shows the furthest Tree
Upon the furthest Slope you know;
It almost speaks to you.

Emily Dickinson

Did you ever wonder: Why is there *something* rather than *nothing*? To quote the well-known question of Stephen Hawking: Why does the universe go through all the bother of existing? Or may I ask: Why did God go through the bother of creating us and this world?

But does God exist? If positive, how do I find Him? How do I find out who am I? What is the purpose of my life?

If God is all-knowing, all-good and all-powerful, why does He allow undeserved suffering?

If God is all-knowing, all-good and all-powerful, why do bad things happen to good people?

How do Christians, religious believers and followers of God respond when non-believers, agnostics or skeptics quote from the daily newspapers those accidents, crimes or natural disasters that resulted in undeserved suffering and untimely deaths?

Dr Rick Warren's bestselling book *The Purpose-Driven Life* emphasizes that life on earth is not about us, that our life on earth is not an accident and that we are born to serve God's purposes.

Perhaps we may wonder: How do we find out that life on earth is not about us, that we are here to serve God's purposes? How do we obtain God's answers to: Why did He create us and this world? How do we obtain God's answers to: What are His purposes for us on earth?

In addition, did you ever experience a sense of meaninglessness? Did you ever experience the need to find your real life purpose?

In the past few years, I liked to discuss with my friends on religious faith, the meaning of life and why bad things happen to good people. To initiate the discussion, I would read the following article [1] which I wrote "*Can You Guess Who am I?*":

> "Can you guess my real identity? Can you guess who am I?
>
> Before you start guessing, please don't be deceived by my masks. I am wearing many social masks at home, at the school, at the workplace and at all types of social gathering. I am trying to show that I am confident, I am happy, I am popular ... But deep inside, I am uncertain.

Please don't be deceived by my smiles and laughter, by my jokes and gossip. I am trying to hide my doubts. I am trying to hide my weariness.

Please don't be deceived by my occasional excitement about life. I am tired of trying to outperform others. I am tired of trying to get ahead and obtain those prizes. I am tired of living my life as if it were a continuous emergency. I am tired of being frightened of losing my job and my friends. How can I find tranquillity? How can I find inner peace?

I am equally tired of not understanding my real needs and goals in life. Is it because I do not truly know my life purpose that I am pursuing external success and sense pleasures, so as to try to fill the emptiness inside?

Please tell me how I can find my life purpose. So many bad things and unhappy events had happened to me. Many of them were unfair. They had eroded my faith in God. Please tell me whether there is a God. Please tell me how I can find Him.

By the way, do you know who am I? Have you guessed who am I? Yes, you are right. I am your neighbor. I am your colleague. I am your boss. I am your cousin. I am your niece. I am your uncle. I am your aunt. I am your brother. I am your sister. I am your child. I am your spouse. I am the everyday man or woman you meet on the street. Yes, I am also you ... Please help me, God."

This book aims to provide useful perspectives, responses and answers to these critical questions. May we begin by revisiting a famous story called "Footprints". I have revised it based on deep insights I received six months ago. This new version reflects the hope, love and truth which God brings to us in the changing seasons of life. To quote Thomas Merton's memorable words in his introduction to the Japanese translation of *The Seven Storey Mountain*: "I seek to speak to you, in some way, as your own self. Who can tell what this may mean? I myself do not know, but if you listen, things will be said that are perhaps not written in this book. And this will be due not to me but to the One who lives and speaks in both ..."

Footprints
(New Version)

Jesus said: "The kingdom of God is within you."

(Luke 17:21)

Saint Teresa of Avila:
"Christ has no body but yours,
no hands and no feet on earth but yours.
Yours are the eyes with which he looks
with compassion on this world.
Yours are the feet with which he walks to do good.
Yours are the hands with which he blesses the world."

Ralph Waldo Emerson: "The soul in man is the background of our being ... From within or from behind, a light shines through us upon things, and makes us aware that we are nothing, but the light is all."

Helen Keller: "I believe that God is in me as the sun is in the color and fragrance of a flower."

Pope John Paul II: "Man's life comes from God."

Mother Teresa: "It is not how much you do, but how much love you put into the doing that matters."

Corrie ten Boom: "God values us not for our strength or our brains, but simply because He has made us."

A middle-aged man dreamed that he had become a spiritual being and that he was walking on a beach together with God, the divine Spirit. They left two trails of footprints in the sand behind them.

Scenes of the man's life flashed across the sky. The man observed that during the pleasant days of his life as shown across the sky, there were two trails of footprints behind them. He knew that God was walking beside him during the pleasant days. But during the difficult days, he observed only one trail of footprints.

Assuming that the one trail of footprints belonged to him and that God had abandoned him during the difficult times, the man enquired why he was left alone to handle the difficulties.

God explained, "You are My precious child. I will never leave you. During your difficult times, when you see one trail of footprints, it was then that I carried you."

The man thanked God. Nevertheless he was perplexed by the answer. Inwardly he reasoned that if God were all-knowing, all-good and all-powerful, why God did not remove or reduce the trials and suffering in his life.

Being all-knowing, God was aware of the man's reasoning. God further explained, "Please realize that I will not let you bear the cross unless it reveals the eternal life within you. I will not let you bear the cross unless it is for your eternal best, unless it contributes to the long-term well-being of humankind."

The man nodded and thanked God. He enquired, "May I know what is my real identity? Do I have a soul?"

"Yes, you have a soul," God said. "Let Me explain. I more than carried you during your difficult times. All along I have been living inside you in the form of spiritual essence. Your body is temporary. Your spiritual essence or your soul is eternal. It is a part of

Me. It is always wholesome, pure and intact. No people and no events in the world can affect it. Nothing can impair it. Nothing can defile it. It is an individualised portion of My essence and cosmic consciousness. It is always wholesome."

The man thanked God and enquired, "Do I return to heaven after I die?"

God continued, "You are My precious child. You are a spiritual being. This is your real identity. You are always connected to My love. Your soul will return to My kingdom when your journey on earth ends."

The man asked, "Thank You for explaining to me my real identity. May I enquire how do I find You? How do I know that You are with me all the time?"

God said, "You can catch glimpses of My presence when you expand your awareness and let go of self-seeking thoughts, feelings and desires. This can happen when you are walking along the seaside, enjoying the warm sunshine, the wide blue sky and the rhythm of the waves. This can happen when you are enjoying the beauty of a sunset or the whispering of a stream or the tranquillity of a lake. This can happen when you are listening to inspiring music or reading a devotional book or poem. This can happen when you are amazed by the splendor of a sunrise or the beauty of a clear night sky filled with glimmering stars.

"Another effective way to expand your awareness is to learn to meditate. It makes you realize that "thoughts, ideas, feelings and desires" are momentary and fleeting. They are flashes of mental energy which arise and pass away. They are not permanent. They are not your selfhood or personality. They are not your real identity.

"Your real identity is a spiritual being. Thus, when you meditate and learn not to chase after momentary thoughts, feelings and desires, slowly you experience mental stillness and tranquillity. Slowly you discover the pure consciousness within you. This pure consciousness is one of My attributes. It is also an attribute of your soul. What you suffered in life, I also suffered and experienced through the pure consciousness living inside you. I am your Living God. I am living inside you during your good days and during your times of suffering and afflictions. By experiencing your suffering and afflictions, I can truly understand."

The man nodded and listened attentively.

God said, "I created the visible universe. I am the Giver of life. I am the Source of your hope and strength. You are My precious child. Nothing can separate you from My love. You can look forward to rejoining Me in heaven when your journey on earth ends. You can be assured that I will transform your suffering into ultimate good. This is how I am truly your heavenly Father."

The man enquired, "May I know what is my life purpose on earth? How do I fulfil it?"

God explained, "You are My precious child on earth serving an eternal purpose. To fulfil this purpose, your soul is combined with a human body. Your waking consciousness is given freedom of choice. Your purpose is to become spiritually aware. In this way your waking consciousness will become receptive to the voice of your soul, the voice of your conscience.

"Gradually you realise the difference between the kind intentions of your soul and selfish desires. You learn to make a commitment to follow the voice of your soul. You choose to be responsible to Me in your daily thoughts, words and deeds. You learn to become spiritually mature. You extend helping hands to the needy. Compassion is realised. This contributes to the moral dimension of life.

"Spiritual maturity is difficult. It requires daily moral commitment. It requires you to choose simplicity, kindness and selfless service. It requires endurance during the trying times and reliance on My strength. It requires you to become My instrument of peace, My vessel of love.

"The Moments of Truth come when you face a deep personal crisis, when you face the loss of your loved ones, when your life is shattered into pieces, when you face death itself. During these Moments, will you choose to follow Me day by day until your last breath?

"When you make this choice and follow Me day by day, despite adversities, despite your doubts, grief, fear and agony, holding on to the belief that I am divine Truth and Goodness, the Significance of these Moments is fulfilled. This is the hard-won, selfless faith the universe and I have been waiting for. This is the precious human resolve, commitment and goodwill the universe and I have been waiting for. It gives birth to and actualizes the quality of moral resolve in the visible world. This is the Significance of why I chose to suffer together with you."

The man thanked God and asked, "I understand that if a person committed a harmful wrongdoing, he would feel guilty. He should repent and seek Your forgiveness. He should find constructive ways to make amends in the remaining days of his life on earth. May I enquire whether there is cosmic justice for those who committed wrongdoing and did not repent. How do these unrepentant people compensate for their harmful wrongdoing if they avoided legal punishment on earth?"

"Please be assured that there is cosmic justice," God explained. "Upon the death of the body, the disembodied soul will be assessed by My Holy Spirit. If this soul during its journey on earth had worked in harmony with the body and its mental states and it had contributed to human well-being, it will be given a choice. It can choose to return to My kingdom or begin another human journey on earth, so as to further contribute to the moral dimension of life.

"If a soul during its journey on earth had endured undeserved suffering and untimely death, it can choose to return to My kingdom or begin another human journey, so as to contribute to the moral dimension of life.

"If a soul during its journey on earth were not able to work in harmony with the body and its mental states, and the human body committed harmful wrongdoing due to selfish desires, upon the death of the body, My Holy Spirit will direct this soul to embark on another or more human journeys on earth. This will provide opportunities where it can contribute to human well-being. When it has sufficiently contributed, it can return to My kingdom."

The man thanked God and asked, "For centuries, humankind sought to find out why God created this world. May I enquire on this age-old question?"

God replied, "It is time for Me to reveal why I created the visible world. Since eternity I have existed. I am the divine Source. I am the Living God. I am the eternal One in the timeless Dimension. I am all-knowing, all-good and all-powerful in the timeless Dimension.

"First, My omniscience in the timeless Dimension is all-sufficient. I know the past, the present and the future. I do not need to create a visible world to complement or prove it. If I wished to create a visible world so as to experience and enjoy it, I can create many types of visible worlds which are peaceful, beautiful and pleasant, without the occurrences of natural and moral evils, without the existence of human beings. Such peaceful and beautiful worlds will be congruent with My knowledge and wisdom. I do not need to create the type of visible world which human beings currently experience which is marked by existential uncertainty and suffering.

"Second, My omnipotence in the timeless Dimension is all-sufficient. I do not need to create a visible world to complement or prove it. If I wished, I can create and eliminate visible worlds without human beings or creatures inhabiting them. If I wished, I can create beautiful and peaceful worlds so as to enjoy them, without the occurrences of natural and moral evils, without the existence of human beings. This is congruent with My power and wisdom.

"Third, being all-good, I am Holiness. I am divine Goodness. But I am also divine Oneness. As divine Oneness in the timeless dimension, I do not have a physical body or bodies. I do not live in a space-time dimension. I am not individualized. I am not embodied.

"In the timeless dimension, it is natural that I do not have the opportunity to experience physical vulnerability and existential uncertainty. I do not have the opportunity to manifest dynamic moral goodness.

"Dynamic moral goodness includes faith, humility, kindness, love, compassion, endurance and selfless service which humankind manifested when they performed compassionate deeds on earth. In addition, dynamic moral goodness requires Me to create individualized human beings or embodied souls. Dynamic moral goodness requires the interactions of individualised, embodied and vulnerable beings in a visible world. They need to experience trials and suffering to become mature. They need to exercise free will inherent in their waking consciousness to make moral decisions and perform good deeds. Thus, it is a natural condition of My divine Oneness that before the creation of the visible world and humankind, I have not yet manifested dynamic moral goodness.

"For eternity, I have remained as divine Oneness. At some point during My eternity, I decided to create a visible world, so as to manifest dynamic moral goodness through My children. I decided that dynamic moral goodness in the visible world is a very valuable attribute which complements My attribute of divine Goodness in the timeless Dimension. I decided to create this stringent challenge for Me and for My children on earth.

"Thus, I created this visible universe and humankind. I individualised My spiritual essence so as to live inside My children. My children and I are moral partners on earth. Through the pure consciousness of their souls, I share the life experiences of My children. Together we experience adversities, trials, and suffering. The purpose is for My children to become spiritually mature. As the voice of their souls, I encourage My children to do good. When the waking consciousness of My children chooses to listen to the voice of their souls, they become spiritually aware. They learn to walk the spiritual path.

"When My children are honest, kind, sympathetic, faithful and compassionate in their daily lives, despite being physically vulnerable and facing existential uncertainty, they are manifesting dynamic moral goodness. When My children resolve to follow Me and choose to do good, despite trials and suffering, they are manifesting high-quality goodness. In these ways I manifest dynamic goodness through My children.

"In human language, this can be called 'God is biting the bullet' theodicy. It means that I have decided that My divine Goodness in the timeless Dimension cannot forever remain untested and unproven. Therefore, during some point in eternity, I have decided to bite the bullet and create a stringent Self-challenge by providing freedom of choice to My children and by allowing the occurrences of natural and moral evils in a visible world. These give rise to existential uncertainty and suffering in the visible world. I have decided to experience and endure such existential uncertainty and suffering together with My children, so as to manifest dynamic moral goodness and contribute to the moral dimension of life.

"In this way, My spiritually mature children are My moral partners. Guided by the voice of their souls, they strive and struggle in the visible world to manifest dynamic moral goodness under the stringent conditions of existential uncertainty and suffering. This attribute of dynamic moral goodness in the visible world complements My attribute of divine Goodness in the timeless dimension."

"Thanks, God. Does this mean that You are not all-knowing and not all-powerful in the visible world?" asked the man.

God replied, "In the timeless Dimension, I am the Source. I am the eternal One. There is enduring peace, beauty, goodness and harmony in the timeless Dimension. I remain and continue to be all-knowing, all-good and all-powerful in the timeless Dimension.

"In contrast, in the visible world, I have chosen to restrict My powers and omniscience. This arises from My decision to bite the bullet and create a visible world which is subject to existential uncertainty and to the occurrences of natural and moral evils. Thus, I have chosen to limit My powers and omniscience in the visible world. I am no longer all-knowing and all-powerful in the visible world.

"The visible world is a small part of the timeless Dimension. I created the laws of the natural sciences and mathematics when creating the visible world. Thereafter, I usually do not intervene directly in the visible world. This allows the occurrences of natural evils. The occurrences of natural evils introduce the crucial element of existential uncertainty into the visible world. They include earthquakes, hurricanes, floods, famines, accidents and diseases. These occur due to the operations of the laws of the sciences on earth.

"Nonetheless, I retain final control of the visible world. I can foresee the range of possible outcomes in the short term or longer term regarding an event or a cluster of events in the visible world. I can choose to occasionally intervene in an event or a cluster of events in the visible world. My decision to intervene is based on the range of possible outcomes of an event or a cluster of events and their long-term impact on the moral dimension of life. I have restricted My power of omniscience in the visible world. If I did not choose to intervene in an event or a cluster of events, I cannot foresee their actual final outcome in the visible world which is subject to the operations of the laws of the sciences and the free will of My children.

"Another aspect is that I have restricted My omniscience and powers in the visible world by providing freedom of choice to My children. I do not intervene in the decisions and choices of My children. I also cannot foresee the final choice of My children regarding an event or a cluster of events facing them. I can only foresee the range of possible outcomes, based on the range of choices facing My children regarding an event or cluster of events. Once My child makes a decision and a choice and acts accordingly, I can better foresee the outcome of his choice.

"I only intervene indirectly by encouraging My children to be conscientious and to do good through the voice of their souls. My children need to listen to the voice of their souls and choose to walk the path of righteousness. However, if some of My children decided to listen to their self-seeking desires and ignore the voice of their souls, they are walking the wrong path. They can commit deeds which harm others. Such moral evils give rise to another layer of existential uncertainty and suffering. On My part, through the voice of their souls, I continue to encourage the wrongdoers and the misguided to repent and urge them to walk the path of righteousness.

"Once I decided to provide freedom of choice to My children, they need to decide and choose their daily conduct and deeds. I have decided to bite the bullet and

I will not intervene in their choices. It is the will and resolve of My children to listen to the voice of their souls and walk the path of righteousness which enable My children and I to become partners on earth to manifest dynamic moral goodness and contribute to the moral dimension of life. In this way, we work towards fulfilling our crucial purpose on earth.

"Thus, I have revealed why I created the visible world and humankind. I am the Giver of life. I am the Source of your hope and strength. You are My precious child. Nothing can separate you from My love. By listening to your conscience and following Me day by day, when your journey on earth ends, you are once again at Home, back in our timeless Garden, with our purpose on earth fulfilled."

The man said, "Thank you, God. May I share these revelations with others?"

God replied, "Please share them with others. You are doing something valuable and beautiful for Me by sharing them with others, with your loved ones and friends. It is crucial to share with them. During their moments of sadness and affliction, during their hours of darkness due to setbacks or unfortunate events, they will remember My words. They will realize that I am always with them. They will realize that they are My precious children and they are always connected to My love. My words will provide them with hope, strength and courage. My words will remind them that they have not lived in vain. As long as they hold on to their faith and belief that I am divine Truth and Goodness, despite existential suffering, they have bravely contributed to the moral dimension of life. They have fulfilled their life purpose. They will rejoin Me in heaven when their journey on earth ends."

Wisdom

Come to me, all you who are weary and burdened, and I will give you rest. Take my yoke upon you and learn from me, for I am gentle and humble in heart, and you will find rest for your souls. For my yoke is easy, and my burden is light.

Matthew 11:28-30

Leave the broken, irreversible past in God's hands, and step out into the invincible future with Him.

Oswald Chambers

Once there was a young evangelist who was always anxious about the future. He worried that he might not have the strength to preach the next day.

One night he dreamed that he met Jesus while he was walking alone. He was returning home after attending a church gathering. He told Jesus about his anxieties.

Jesus consoled him and said that He understood his anxieties. He offered the following advice. First, He told the young man to repeat His words from "John 14:27" whenever he felt anxious: "Peace I leave you. My peace I give to you." This would calm him, enabling him to experience tranquillity and sustenance from God.

Second, Jesus told the young man to repeat these words whenever he lacked confidence: "I can do all things through Christ who strengthens me." (Philippians 4:13) This would remind him that God would always provide him with strength whenever he needed it. He ought to remind himself that God is all-knowing, all-good and all-powerful, that God is the Creator of this universe. He may feel weak, but God is forever strong.

Third, Jesus advised the young man to let go of his worries by learning to live one day at a time, one moment at a time, in the strength of God. Jesus informed him that he could deepen his faith in God by affirming these words whenever he experienced doubts: "What God decides for me is for my long-term good and for my eternal best. He is mainly concerned about my love for Him, my love and compassion for the people I interact with, and my sincerity to assist the needy. As long as I love God, as long as I am sincere in helping others for worthwhile purposes, I have done good for the day. It is alright that I am not the best performer. Love, sincerity, honesty, humility and compassion are much more valuable in the eyes of God."

Fourth, Jesus advised the young man to pray every morning the following prayers. They will remind him that life in this world is temporary, that only God can fulfil his spiritual needs by providing him with love and peace. Jesus lifted his right hand and gently moved it. The words of these prayers appeared across the sky:-

Saint Teresa's prayer :

Lord, please make me realize that
You are always with me.
Your love for me is constant.
Please make me understand
that nothing can disturb me,
nothing can make me afraid.

Please make me realise
that all things in the world are passing,
all things in the world are temporary.
Only You and Your love are eternal.
As You are forever with me, I do not lack anything.
You are sufficient for all my needs.

Saint Francis' prayer:

Lord, make me an instrument of Your peace:
where there is hatred, let me bring Your love,
where there is injury, let me bring Your pardon,
where there is discord, let me bring Your harmony,
where there is doubt, let me bring faith,
where there is despair, let me bring hope,

and where there is darkness, let me bring light.

Lord, make me an instrument of Your peace:
Grant that I may seek to console than to be consoled,
that I seek to understand than to be understood,
that I seek to love than to be loved.
For it is by forgetting the self that one finds;
it is by giving that one receives;
it is by forgiving that one is forgiven;
it is by dying that one awakens to eternal life.

A new prayer from Jesus (by Merton Lee):

Dear God, please make me realize that You are the Creator of this cosmos. All events are ultimately under Your control. You are my eternal strength and stronghold. Although I may feel weak, You are forever strong. I can rely on Your strength, wisdom and compassion.

Please make me realize my real identity as Your child. I contain Your individualized spiritual essence which is my soul. My soul comes from You. I am always connected to Your love. You are always inside me in the form of spiritual essence and pure consciousness.

Please make me realize that my body is temporary, but my soul is eternal. It is timeless. It is always wholesome, pure and intact. Nothing can affect it. Nothing can impair it. Thus, my life on earth is a journey, a pilgrimage to Your Holy Kingdom. You will decide whether I will live one day more or less on earth. When You decide that it is time to bring me home, my soul will return to Your kingdom to enjoy eternal harmony.

One of the attributes of my soul is pure consciousness. I can experience pure consciousness when I am mentally still and tranquil. I can learn meditation to experience tranquillity and inner peace. This enables me to realize the priceless gifts which You have given to me, namely my spiritual essence as well as the gifts of wisdom, understanding, compassion, love and peace. Please help me to share these gifts with others and help me to awaken them to Your gifts.

May I submit to the guidance of Your Hands and the Holy Spirit day by day. May I rely on Your decisions which are always for my eternal best. Please help me to remain humble, upright and God-reliant during moments of triumph or defeat, happiness or sorrow, clarity or confusion, strength or affliction. May I be very grateful and realize the preciousness of Your gifts. They are the foundation of healthy self-esteem and inner peace. Your gifts are sufficient for all my needs. I do not need to chase after external success and worldly recognition. I can let go of selfish motives and self-seeking desires. I can rise above the need to impress others.

Please guide me to choose simplicity, non-attachment and prudence. Please inspire me to be conscientious, kind and helpful. Please make me realize that You are my genuine lifelong Employer. I cannot become jobless. I am always employed by

You. I am always Your instrument to do good. I am serving God by performing little acts of kindness, by extending an encouraging word to others day by day. In this way I have done good in my lifetime. In this way I am fulfilling my purpose in life day by day. I have not lived in vain. I have not suffered in vain. By enduring life's adversities and walking the path of righteousness day by day, I am deepening my faith in God.

Please make me realize that my life purpose is to become spiritually aware and mature, that I am Your partner on earth to manifest dynamic moral goodness. Please guide me to serve You with humility and contentment day by day, so that I can live my life at my own pace, learning useful skills and knowledge to contribute to the well-being of my loved ones and others. If I were afflicted with illness and became a care-receiver, please continue to strengthen my faith and help me realize that my illness can provide opportunity for others to assist me and show compassion to me.

Please make me realize that I might have died yesterday. Thus, help me to treasure each new day. Help me to regard each new day as Your bonus gift to me. Every day is a bonus for me to show my love for You, to show my love and appreciation to my family and to the people around me. Please make me realize that the people around me are seeking for love and acceptance. Please guide me to extend compassionate words and deeds to others day by day, so that I can do something beautiful for You. Thank you very much, God. [2]

Pilgrimage On Earth

Sometimes people get the mistaken notion that spirituality is a separate department of life. Rightly understood, it is a vital awareness that pervades all realms of our being.

Brother David Steindl-Rast

I was born in July 1969 in Singapore. I was born in humble circumstances. My father did not have a stable job while my mother was a full-time housewife taking care of my two siblings, our grandparents and me. Thus, I considered myself very fortunate to be able to attend school to receive formal education.

In addition, I was born with fragile health and occasional back pain due to curvature of my spine. I did not have the energy and strength to participate in sports. During my school days, apart from school text books, I did not have money to buy other books. Thus, I frequented the school and public libraries, reading a range of subjects.

From the age of fourteen onwards, I became interested in the meaning of life. I began to read the Bible and the wisdom literature of the major religions. I also became a Christian and accepted Jesus Christ as the Lord.

As the years passed by, I discovered the usefulness of practising the wisdom teaching. Besides providing me with positive thinking, they inculcated in me the value of service. They inspired me to serve noble causes. By undertaking meditation, my health slowly improved. I was able to complete two and a half years of national service in the Republic of Singapore Navy.

I did well in my academic studies. By the age of twenty-three, I obtained a Bachelor's degree in Philosophy and Economics at the National University of Singapore. I started to work part-time. In the next three years, I obtained a Master's degree in Accountancy and another Master's degree in Business Administration via distance learning. At the age of twenty-six, I joined a public sector organisation as a full-time finance manager. For the next eighteen years, I devoted my best years to public service.

Thus, for three decades, I have been studying, reflecting on and practising the key insights of the perennial wisdom of the major religions. As I reach forty-four years of age, after serving more than twenty years in the public sector including national service and after being married for seventeen years and as a father of two children, I deeply appreciate that practising these key insights has enabled me to accept life's difficulties.

In addition, over the years, I experienced the deaths of loved ones, friends and colleagues owing to illnesses or accidents. Those dark days made me feel keenly the preciousness and vulnerability of life. They made me feel my deep need for God. I realised that only the Creator could provide me with spiritual strength to handle adversities.

Sad days and dark moments also made me realise that adversities and setbacks grow the seeds of spiritual qualities within us. They made us humble, sympathetic and compassionate. Gradually we realise the importance of becoming God-centered and God-reliant.

Further, from age forty-two onwards, due to high workload, my back pain recurred, together with gastric pain and ailments. There were instances when my back pain radiated and extended to become chest pain and breathlessness. The doctors prescribed painkillers. On my part, I lengthened my daily meditation and took herbal medication for many months. Slowly my health improved. These experiences deepened my empathy for the sick and needy. I contributed more regularly a part of my income to charitable organisations which include the Red Cross, a local hospital for the poor and the Children's Cancer Foundation. I could more deeply understand the words of Dietrich Bonhoeffer: "We must learn to regard people less in the light of what they do or omit to do, and more in the light of what they suffer."

For many years, I have also been contemplating and reflecting on: *Who are we? Why are we here? What is the meaning of life? Why does the world exist?* I experienced deep insights in year 2012. As a humble messenger of God, may I convey His revelations and messages in this book.

In the past ten years, I have been discussing with my friends on religious faith. One of their main reasons for rejecting God was that they could not accept the notion of an all-knowing, all-good and all-powerful God who allows undeserved suffering and untimely death. I hope His messages in the final part of this book will answer their questions.

On my part, when I discussed with my friends on religious faith, I liked to tell the following true story. It reflects an exemplary commitment to do something beautiful for God:

Many years ago a pastor named Russell Conwell saw a little girl crying near the door of a small church. It was over-crowded and she could not enter it.

"I cannot attend Sunday School ..." she wept as the pastor walked by. The kind-hearted pastor took her inside and found a place for her in the Sunday school class.

The child called Hattie was so touched that she went to bed that night worrying about those children who had no place to worship God. She began saving her money, so as to contribute towards building a larger Sunday school.

Over a period of two years Hattie saved 57 cents before she contracted diphtheria and died. It was difficult for a poor girl to save 57 cents in the 1880s in the United States. Her parents gave the money to pastor Conwell, explaining to him their daughter's reason for saving the money.

The girl's devotion deeply moved pastor Conwell. For two years Hattie had sacrificially saved her offering of love. Pastor Conwell instantly knew what he would do. He repeated the story of the girl's big-hearted love and devotion to God. He challenged his deacons to raise money for a larger building.

A newspaper also published this event. A realtor was so touched by it that he offered a significant parcel of land. When he realised that the church could not afford it, he offered it for 57 cents. Church members and

Christians from other places also donated. Within five years the little girl's gift had increased to $250,000 -- a huge sum at that time.

Hattie's gift and her pastor's determination resulted in today's Temple Baptist Church attended by thousands and the Sunday School building which can house hundreds of Sunday school children where no child need to be left outside. In one of the rooms of this building may be seen the picture of the little girl Hattie whose love for God is remembered forever. [3]

Waiting

Doing something beautiful for God
and becoming beautiful doing it ...
Timothy I 2:10 (The Message)

Let's do something beautiful for God.
Mother Teresa

Whatever you do, work at it with all your heart, as working for the Lord, not for men ...
Colossians 3:23

Several years ago I attended a gathering of Christian friends. We noticed that one of the children was blind. She was eleven years old and had been born blind. But she appeared serene, bright and cheerful. She could play the piano very well. We admired her buoyant spirit.

Suddenly a boy said, “I feel so sorry for you. You are so pitiful ...”

The adults quickly informed the boy not to say indiscreet things. To our surprise, the blind girl replied cheerfully, “I am not pitiful. In fact I consider myself very fortunate.”

All the adults and their healthy children were amazed by her optimism and positive attitude. She explained, “Although I am blind, I can speak, hear, taste, smell and do many things. I love singing, listening to music and playing the piano. I can tell stories to other children about my blessings which are provided by God. Recently I participated in a charity event by playing the piano. I was glad to contribute my part to raising funds for the poor.”

All the adults and I were speechless. We could clearly discern her kind-hearted soul through her smiles.

She continued, “Most importantly, I have wonderful parents. I love listening to my mother telling wonderful stories from the Bible. I know that Jesus Christ always loves me. I pray to Him every day. I give thanks for all the wonderful gifts and abilities He has given me. Now I wish to share my secret with you. The reason why I consider myself to be very fortunate is that when I pass away and return to His kingdom, when I open my eyes, I shall see the beauty of heaven, the smiles of angels and the Face of our Saviour ... ”

This girl’s resilient spirit reminded me of poet John Milton who was blind when he wrote *Paradise Lost*. In his poem “On His Blindness”, Milton provided a profound meaning to the need for ‘waiting’ -- humble, reverent and patient waiting for God’s direction and for the unfolding of His purpose:-

When I consider how my light is spent
Ere half my days in this dark world and wide,
And that one talent which is death to hide

Lodg'd with me useless, though my soul more bent
To serve therewith my Maker, and present
My true account, lest he returning chide,
"Doth God exact day-labour, light denied?"
I fondly ask. But Patience, to prevent
That murmur, soon replies: "God doth not need
Either man's work or his own gifts: who best
Bear his mild yoke, they serve him best. His state
Is kingly; thousands at his bidding speed
And post over land and ocean without rest:
They also serve who only stand and wait."

Waiting was common in my life. For example, during my National Service days, I was posted to a new camp after I was promoted to Lance Corporal. Accordingly, from Monday to Saturday at 5.15 am in the morning, I travelled on a bus for an hour from my home to the new camp. Thereafter I trudged slowly up a steep hill for 30 minutes before reaching my camp. I was usually panting and sweating heavily by the time I reached the top of the hill. This continued for more than one year before I completed my national service. At that time I did not enjoy the daily toil, although it gradually strengthened my health. I was more eager to enrol in the local university to study Philosophy and Economics. Now, years later, I realised that God was cultivating the habit of 'patient waiting' in me, as I tend to be impatient during my younger days.

As I reach mid-forties in age, I realise that spiritual growth takes time. Catching a glimpse of God's purpose takes time. When we begin to walk the spiritual path, we may experience moments of joyful awakening. They arise from the release of pent-up unhappiness. Initially they can make us feel lighter. They can make us feel big-hearted. But these feelings arise and pass away. Thereafter we have to persevere to follow God day by day. We learn to become responsible to God in our daily thoughts, words and deeds. No one can make this daily decision for us. No one can make this daily choice for us. This is the significance of having free will. This is the responsibility of having free will inherent in our ordinary waking consciousness. We have to decide. We have to choose to follow the kind intentions of the soul. We have to choose not to be driven by selfish motives.

May I share an unforgettable story called *The Giving Tree* by Shel Silverstein which I have summarized here [4].

Once there was a tree and she loved a little boy. Every day they would play together. He would climb up her trunk and swing from her branches and eat her apples. They were very happy.

As time passed by, the boy became a young man who needed money. At first the tree gave him her apples. When this did not meet the needs of the young man, the tree gave him her branches and finally her trunk. Thereafter the young man travelled overseas. He did not visit the tree for a long time which had become a stump.

Many years later, the man returned as an old man. The tree told him that it had nothing left to give him. The man explained that his teeth did not have the strength to bite apples. His arms did not have the strength to swing on the branches. He also did not have the strength to travel to other places. He would be contented to sit on the stump and relive their memories. Thus, the tree and the man became happy again.

In our journey through life, are we thankful to people who have contributed to our well-being? Are we thankful to our spiritual ancestors who brought awakening to the world and improved the well-being of humankind? Did we give deep thanks to Jesus Christ who awakened us to the love of God?

Did we express thankfulness to God for giving us life, for giving us intelligence, understanding and wisdom? Did we express thankfulness to God for giving us a range of abilities which enables us to appreciate and contribute to life? Did we develop a contented and grateful heart? Did we realise that in choosing to extend a kind thought, word or deed to others during a day, that will be a fruitful day? Did we realise that God is the ultimate Giving Tree, patiently waiting for us to grow, to become mature, to catch glimpses of His eternal purpose?

Bringing Cheerful Tunes to Heaven

During my school days, owing to my fragile health and occasional back pain, I sympathised more readily with the sick and needy. Thus, I participated in different kinds of fund-raising activities for the poor. For example, on several occasions, a few of my classmates and I volunteered to sell stickers to the public so as to seek their donations for charity purposes. Early in the morning, we were each given an empty tin can and we travelled to the shopping centers and bus interchanges to seek donations from the public. Although it was tiring to walk and stand the whole day around those busy areas, approaching people for donations, it was satisfying when our tin cans were filled with coins in the evening. We returned to our school by bus and handed over the cans to our teachers to be passed to a local charity.

In a small way, at that young age, my classmates and I were learning to be helpful towards the less fortunate in our society. Guided by the Holy Spirit, we were watering the seeds of compassion within us. To quote Mother Teresa, it is crucial to do small things with love, to perform little acts of kindness day by day. In this way we are doing something beautiful for God.

In the past few months, as inspired by the Holy Spirit, I had a vision. In performing acts of kindness day by day, when our journey on earth ends and we return to heaven, the Holy Spirit will hand a beautiful box to each of us. When we open this box, cheerful tunes and rays of rainbow will appear and travel across the heavenly kingdom. These cheerful tunes and rays of rainbow come from the acts of kindness that we had performed on earth. They complement those diverse Symphonies and Bridges of Rainbows that we experience in heaven.

But what is astonishing is when the Holy Spirit whispers to us, saying "Please look and hear carefully ..." Slowly we realize that many of those gracious Symphonies and Bridges of Rainbows are made up of all the cheerful tunes and rays of rainbow brought back by the many souls who returned from their earthly journeys. Without their tunes and rays of rainbow, there will be lesser Symphonies and Bridges of Rainbows in heaven. Perhaps this is a poetic way to develop some understanding of God's decision that it is very valuable to manifest dynamic moral goodness on earth because it complements divine Goodness in the eternal dimension.

> *... you'll do best by filling your minds and meditating on things true, noble, reputable, authentic, compelling, gracious—the best, not the worst; the beautiful, not the ugly; things to praise, not things to curse. Put into practice what you learned from me, what you heard and saw and*

realized. Do that, and God, who makes everything work together, will work you into his most excellent harmonies.

Philippians 4:8-9

May I share a real story about a girl called "little Annie". Many years ago there was a girl known as "little Annie". She became partially blind at the age of five due to bacterial eye infection. Her family was too poor to provide her with medical treatment. Her mother died when she was eight and her father subsequently abandoned her.

Thus, little Annie was sent to the state poor house where she was kept in an over-crowded room and exposed to mentally ill adults. This worsened her defiant personality. The caregivers at the poor house regarded her as being hopelessly defiant and she received little care and attention.

Fortunately one of the caregivers refused to regard little Annie as being hopeless. She felt that there was hope for every child of God. She decided to communicate hope and love to little Annie. Gradually they became friends and little Annie became less defiant.

Little Annie longed to attend school. A few years later when she was fourteen, the Head of the State Board of Charities, Franklin Sanborn, visited the poor house for an inspection. Annie courageously walked up to him and requested to go to school. That year she left the poor house and entered the Perkins Institution for the Blind in Boston. She also underwent eye surgery which partially restored her vision. Six years later at the age of twenty, Annie graduated from the Perkins Institution, informing her schoolmates that "duty bids her to go into active life."

Many years later the Queen of England was pinning her country's highest award onto Helen Keller, the famous writer who inspired millions, despite being blind and deaf since young. The Queen asked her how did she overcome so many difficulties and accomplish so much, although she was blind and deaf. Helen Keller replied that her accomplishments could be attributed to the love and devotion of Anne Sullivan ("little Annie"). If not for Anne Sullivan, the name 'Helen Keller' would remain unknown. [5]

This real life story reflected how the kind-hearted deeds of the caregiver and Franklin Sanford positively changed the life of little Annie. In turn little Annie helped to develop the potential of Helen Keller. Subsequently Helen Keller inspired millions through her writings.

Thus, the far-reaching impact of every kind-hearted deed cannot be under-estimated. Only God knows the long-term outcomes. As emphasized by Romans 8:28, "All things work for the good of those who love God and are called according to His purposes ..."

If we extend a kind thought, word or deed to another person each day, that will be a fruitful day in the eyes of God. If we hold on to our faith and belief that God is divine Truth and Goodness, despite our daily trials and suffering, we are contributing our part to the moral dimension of life. In this way we are fulfilling our life purpose day by day. Thus, we have not lived in vain. This is reflected in my favourite poem "I Shall Not Live In Vain" by Emily Dickinson:

If I can stop one heart from breaking
I shall not live in vain.
If I can ease one life the aching
Or cool one pain

Or help one fainting robin
Unto his nest again
I shall not live in vain.

May we realize that we have not lived in vain, that we have not suffered in vain as long as we hold on to our faith in God and follow Him day by day. May I quote the immortal words of Helen Keller. Her profound faith in God has inspired and encouraged so many of us in the different seasons of life.

> *They took away what should have been my eyes, but I remembered Milton's Paradise. They took away what should have been my ears. Beethoven came and wiped away my tears. They took away what should have been my tongue, but I had talked with God when I was young. He would not let them take away my soul. Possessing that I still possess the whole.*
>
> *I am conscious of a soul -- a sense that lifts me above the narrow, cramping circumstances of my life.*

Character cannot be developed in ease and quiet. Only through experience of trial and suffering can the soul be strengthened, ambition inspired and success achieved.

For three things I thank God every day of my life: thanks that He has vouchsafed my knowledge of His works; deep thanks that He has set in my darkness the lamp of faith; deep, deepest thanks that I have another life to look forward to -- a life joyous with light and flowers and heavenly song.

If the blind put their hands in God's, they find their way more surely than those who see but do not have faith.

I believe that life is given to us so that we may grow in love, and I believe that God is in me as the sun is in the color and fragrance of a flower.

Helen Keller

When Pebbles Share The Mystery [6]
(On reading the poem "Dover Beach")

Those pebbles in morning light,
they prefer living in that kind of spring
less touched by time.
Perhaps they share the Mystery
or can share their mystery with us.

Are they timeless siblings?
Are they another kind of holograms
containing a piece, a glimpse of our Creator?
Are they crystallized droplets of God's tears –
tears of hope, resolve, healing, renewal?

Or they half-speak, half-disclose to us
only because they have been baptized
by the ancient waves,
by the raw visible world,
by His voice from the sea.

Or together with the waves
they resonate those birth pangs,

growth, waning, and revival of human faith,
those epoch-making conflicts, awesome sacrifices
at the world's naked shingles and hallowed grounds.

Or the immemorial waves
have dissolved blood, toil, tears, and sweat --
the pebbles sanctified further
into light-reflecting prisms:
glimpses of His greater vision.

Or pebbles all along are part of the Mystery,
beckoning at the meek,
for in tempering human wills,
inner kingdoms are tamed,
bearing fruits nurtured by the Spirit,
some with the scent of hidden seaside laurels ...

Those pebbles in evening light,
the earthly self has since been emptied,
to be filled with their blessing,
a kind of special blessing
coming from these offspring of mythical stones,
so at home with the nuances of sunrays

while distilling secrets of the Deep ...

Is the immense blueness before us,
an aimless Experiment
or out-of-proportioned Accident?
Are those seagulls, pelicans, and sparrows,
ventures of an impersonal Chaos
or an untrammelled Free Will?

Beyond the veil of Chaos,
beyond red claws and battle cries,
do we sense *something* which Death's scythe
cannot smell, taste or touch?
Is that *something* providing
life to our bodies and souls?
Are our bodies and souls,
revived by wise breezes,
nudged to converse with the One?

Did God resolve to create
a stringent Self-challenge,
akin to *biting the bullet*,
giving us free will

to the extent that we can reject Him,
to such depth that we can denounce Him ...
so that when whispers of the Mystery reach us,
we awaken to greater depths,
where His love flows
beyond those special spring mornings,
beyond those rivers of time,
beyond our surprises of being born?

Can we stand on tiptoes on the golden sand;
can we climb a tree, a hill, a vantage point,
to reach that warm sunlit height
of our feelings, sensing, awareness,
trying to look over the rim of the sea,
hoping to catch that gleam from the Source ...
or simply contented to be surprised
by the unique *life*
already glowing, breathing, blinking
on our suntanned faces?
Perhaps inside,
somewhere somehow we know
those glowing, breathing, blinking
are already coming

from beyond the rim of the sea.

Or can we enter the thin places between heartbeats,
glimpsing the inner kingdom of Saint Francis,
before disappearing ...
becoming *Life's* children once again,
as precious as the eyes of that evening light,
finding new, old and long-lost friends,
memories, dreams, and joy
among the waters, waves, pebbles, and seashells ...
until beyond our wishes for something more,
beyond poem-writing and reverie,
we finally sense their mystery,
eager to tell us
how to discover,
how to be amazed
by the many-splendored thing,
a blue sea with sunlight sparkling on it,
because within it,
when we are allowed a glimpse,
is the *life-giving Presence.*

Merton Lee

A Summer of Strength
(Sharing His Messages of Strength,
Courage and Self-Transcendence)

Conclusion

(The Prelude)

It was a Summer's night, a close warm night,
Wan, dull and glaring, with a dripping mist
Low-hung and thick that cover'd all the sky,
Half threatening storm and rain; but on we went
Uncheck'd, being full of heart and having faith
In our tried Pilot ...

William Wordsworth

Faith means that whether I am visibly delivered or not, I will stick to my belief that God is love.

Oswald Chambers

As you walk through the valley of the unknown, you will find the footprints of Jesus both in front of you and beside you.

Dr Charles Stanley

A truth-seeker said to God, "The good I did to others was soon forgotten."

God replied, "Please continue to do good because I remember."

The seeker said, "The kindness I extended to others was regarded with doubts and distrust."

God replied, "Please continue to be kind because I understand."

The seeker said, "The love and care I showed to others went unnoticed."

God replied, "Please continue to show love and care because I am aware."

The seeker said, "Thank you, God, for enlightening me. But I observe that the worthwhile deeds I performed in the past which helped others were not permanent. They did not last."

God replied, “Be assured that all worthwhile deeds are honoured in heaven. Thus, please continue to perform them.”

The seeker said, “I could only carry out little acts of kindness in my lifetime and I am a nobody in the eyes of the world.”

God replied, “Please continue to perform little acts of kindness in your lifetime because they are the most beautiful things in My eyes, because you are always My precious child, because you are always Somebody in My eyes.”

The seeker asked, “Every now and then, despite my best efforts, I yielded to pride, greed and desire for sense pleasure.”

God replied, “As an embodied being, you cannot outgrow temptations. Thus you need to maintain vigilance at all times. If you stumbled or made mistakes, please repent sincerely, seek My forgiveness, make amends and move on with life.”

The seeker asked, "Why is my life filled with difficulties and setbacks? Why am I bearing the cross in many days of my life?"

God replied, "Please realise that I will not let you bear the cross unless it reveals the eternal life within you, unless it is for your eternal best. Please realise that you are My precious child. Nothing can separate you from My love. I am always with you. When your journey on earth ends, you will rejoin Me in heaven."

The seeker said, "If I faced temptations, if I felt anxious, sad and fearful, what should I should?"

God replied, "Your thoughts and feelings of anxiety, sadness and fear are temporary. They are flashes of mental energy which arise and pass away. Your body is also temporary. But your soul or your spiritual essence is eternal. Your soul comes from Me. It is always wholesome, pure and intact. Nothing can affect it. Your soul will return to My kingdom when your journey on earth ends. If you faced temptations, if you felt anxious, sad and fearful, please repeat these words until once again you are aware that you are always connected to My Love: *"Peace of God ... Forgiveness of God ... Power of God ... Love of God ..."* You may feel weak at this moment, but your Creator God is forever strong. I created this visible universe. It reflects only a small part of My Power and Strength. Thus if you repeat these words, you will be filled with spiritual strength and courage which come from Me. They enable you to endure the difficulties of life until I decide to bring you home to My kingdom."

The seeker said, "Thank you, God. May I ask what is my life purpose on earth?"

God replied, "To become spiritually aware and do something beautiful for Me."

The seeker said, "How do I begin?"

God replied, "You will be doing something beautiful for Me by sharing this message with others ..."

The Tree of Adversities

Once there was an old giant tree in a forest near to a village. It produced flowers and fruits that were bitter and ugly. The villagers called it the Tree of Adversities. They told their children not to go near it, saying that it was useless and did not bring any benefit.

One year, during a hot summer, a group of villagers became sick. They coughed seriously and felt dizzy. For two months the medicine men of the village could not find a cure.

One of the medicine men decided to search the nearby forest for new herbs. After searching for several days and without finding new herbs, he was on the verge of giving up when he saw the Tree of Adversities. He rested under its shade and watched a squirrel eating its bitter fruits.

"Perhaps these fruits can be useful," he thought. He picked up several ripe fruits and went home to cook them. One of the patients volunteered to drink the soup. Surprisingly he recovered a few days later. Thereafter the other patients drank the soup and also recovered. [1]

Adversities are valuable teachers. Their bitterness contains healing properties. If we encountered "trees of adversities" in the form of difficult people and challenging situations, we ought to reflect on what type of lessons we can learn from them.

For example, did their 'bitterness' disclose an unhealthy attachment to external success? Did their 'bitterness' disclose an inflated sense of self-importance and pride? Did their 'bitterness' disclose that we have placed worldly recognition before our commitment to serve God? Did their 'bitterness' prompt us to assess whether we have discovered our real identity as children of God or are we driven by discontent, envy and greed? Did their 'bitterness' deepen our patience, sympathy, understanding and compassion?

Over the years I realize that adversities are formidable healing forces. They help to break those equally formidable husks which formed within us over the years -- the husks of self-centeredness and pride. These are formed by the negative mental conditioning of secular societies that emphasise external success. They are formed when we are not aware of the importance of practising the perennial wisdom. They are formed when we reinforce self-seeking thoughts.

These husks have trapped us. They trap us by restricting and narrowing our spiritual awareness. They hinder us from finding the Source of life. They deceive us into thinking that life is a zero-sum game, that others are rivals seeking to take away limited external prizes. They deceive us into thinking that life is a continuous emergency, that we must keep fighting to outperform others. Anxiety and unease become our constant companions. They create a scarcity mindset, depriving us of inner peace.

Adversities are wake-up calls. They help to break these husks. When these husks give way and are discarded, we are prompted to discover our real identity as children of God. We are prompted to discover our need for God, for His love and sustenance.

A Lifelong Experiment

At the age of thirty-two, Buckminster Fuller encountered a series of business failures. One late evening he found himself contemplating suicide for several hours at the edge of Lake Michigan.

After careful reflections, he decided to challenge himself. From that day onwards, he regarded himself as having died that night. He would live each new day as a gift from the Universe. He sought to embark on an experiment during the remaining days of his life to find out what an individual could do to contribute to the well-being of humanity. He kept asking the question: What is it on this planet that needs doing that I know something about, that probably won't happen unless I take responsibility for it?

The rest became history. He lived to the ripe old age of eighty-seven. He became a systems theorist, an author of thirty books and a well-known inventor which included the geodesic dome. [2]

This real life story enables me to better appreciate the significance of the precept "Please learn to die before we die." By letting go of the desire for personal advancement, we free up much energies previously used to defend, support and protect the illusory ego. These energies can be channelled to assist the needy.

In addition, we realise that egoistic pride, thoughts and feelings are flashes of mental energies. They are fleeting. They arise and pass away. They are not solid entities. In softening and letting go of egoistic pride, we can more readily discern our past mistakes, wrongdoing and selfish choices. We learn to repent, pray for God's forgiveness, find appropriate ways to make amends and move on with life. To quote C. S. Lewis: "A Christian is not a man who never goes wrong, but a man who is enabled to repent and pick himself up and begin over again after each stumble."

Inner Wealth

Blessed is the man who finds wisdom,
the man who gains understanding,
for she is more profitable than silver
and yields better returns than gold.
Proverbs 3: 13-14

The rooster's eyes were somber and shiny-black with anger as I taunted it with a stick. When the rooster refused to retreat, I assumed the posture of a knight and began brandishing the stick in the air and shouted, "Flee or else you'll get a beating ..."

The rooster was adamant. It did not move. It was eyeing and assessing me.

Frustrated I picked up several stones and threw them at the rooster. The stones hit its silky-red feathers.

My tactic succeeded. The rooster turned with fright and scurried away.

Thrilled and triumphant, I began chasing it across the field, behaving like a victorious knight. While I was enjoying this prankish act, the rooster suddenly turned around. Cackling aggressively, it pecked at me with its beak.

Barely five years old, I was shocked out of my wits. Forgetting that I could defend myself with the stick, I mindlessly flung it away and ran towards my grandfather, who was my playmate during our occasional morning walks.

"Grandpa, help me!" I shrieked.

My grandfather, who was talking to a neighbour, rushed forward and picked me up in his arms, saving me from the wrathful rooster.

My grandfather's embrace, the consoling tenor of his voice, his lean features and compassionate eyes made me feel blessed.

Regaining a sense of bravery, I indicated to my grandfather that I wished to retrieve the knight's stick and re-conquer that rebellious rooster.

My grandfather shook his head and said, “No more prankish act. If you were a rooster and a boy were to hurt you with stones and a stick, how would you feel? Do not do to others what you do not wish others to do to you.”

Although this incident happened nearly forty years ago, it stayed fresh in my memory.

Anyone who proposes to do good must not expect people to roll stones out of his way, but must accept his lot calmly, even if they roll a few more upon it.
Albert Schweitzer

Before the Second World War, my grandfather owned many acres of plantations in Malaysia and was very wealthy. He inherited his wealth in his twenties from his father, a successful merchant.

An honest and kind-hearted person, my grandfather was far from being a shrewd strategy-minded businessman. Various family sources informed me that owing to economic downturns and the upheavals caused by the Second World War in Southeast Asia, my grandfather lost all his wealth in his early forties, when my father was only a boy and I was not born yet ...

My grandfather passed away peacefully at the age of eighty-one when I was twelve years old. That was many years ago. Being his favorite grandson, we shared many happy moments together, like playing Chinese chess, reading, rearing various kinds of tropical fish and planting diverse types of orchids in the backyard. An avid philatelist in his younger days, my grandfather taught me how to collect stamps and differentiate the national identities of numerous stamps. I missed him a lot.

When I was a boy, I used to watch my grandfather watering his orchid plants. In some days he used a brush to scrub away the numerous little dots of parasitic algae that were sticking onto the stems, branches and leaves of the orchid plants.

On one occasion I was playing in the backyard and knocked down an orchid plant. Instead of rebuking me, my grandfather patiently cleaned up the spot where I had accidentally knocked down the clay pot which housed the orchid plant. Sensing his patience and forgiving heart, I calmed down and silently assisted him in sweeping away the lumps of earth and small pieces of stones and charcoal that supported the roots of the plant. Thereafter we replaced the plant into a clay pot that contained the correct proportions of earth, fertilizer, stones, and charcoal. When we had completed our task, my grandfather sat on a stool and rested.

"Why do we need to scrub away the little parasites? Mother told me that they will grow again soon." I recalled asking him.

His amiable face lightened into a smile.

"Scrubbing away the little parasites can prevent them from destroying the leaves or blocking sufficient sunlight from reaching the plants. When we are young, each of us is similar to this tender orchid plant. Our parents need to take care of us, so that we grow taller and stronger each day. The nurturing efforts of our parents are their way to contribute to life. In turn the nurturing efforts deepen the sense of commitment, patience and responsibility in our parents."

At that young age I could not understand the meaning of these words. Now, years later, their wisdom sparkles ...

The great lessons I learn from my grandfather are to take things easy; to let go of external failures; to accept "unacceptable" life changes; to re-center and move on with honesty and integrity. Imagine if we lost fifty thousand dollars in the stock market or in a business venture, most of us will be sad and depressed. If we lost one hundred thousand dollars, we will be in despair. What if we lost our entire wealth? That was literally what happened to my grandfather.

Losing all his wealth in his early forties, my grandfather did not lose his sense of inner balance. Re-centering himself, he started a small retail shop. For the next twenty years, he worked hard to eke out a living to raise five children. He remained an affable and helpful person. Various sources told me that despite his poverty, he continued to extend helping hands to needy relatives to tide them over their difficulties during those lean years after the Second World War.

Looking back at the long life of my grandfather, I realize how big-hearted and resilient he was in accepting failures, in accepting and looking beyond the adversities of life. His compassion and profound sense of letting go left an indelible impression on me. He had unearthed inner wealth far more precious than external gold.

> *Here is a rule to remember when anything tempts you to feel bitter: not "This is a misfortune", but "To bear this worthily is good fortune".*
>
> *Marcus Aurelius*

> *To laugh often and love much; to win the respect of intelligent persons and the affection of children; to earn the approval of honest critics and endure the betrayal of false friends; to appreciate beauty; to find the best in others; to give of one's self without the slightest thought of return; to have accomplished a task, whether by a healthy child, a rescued soul, a garden patch, or a redeemed social condition; to have played and laughed with enthusiasm and exaltation; to know that even one life has breathed easier because you have lived; this is to have succeeded.* *Ralph Waldo Emerson*

During younger days, I was fascinated by the lives of rich and successful people. I studied their autobiographies and biographies. In my lifetime, I came into contact with many wealthy and successful people. Some of them inherited their wealth. Some became rich through self-education and perseverance. Others became rich by capitalizing on fortuitous events.

Some earned their first million while in the prime of their life and sustained their wealth to the end. Others earned their first million in their twenties, but became insolvent before they reached thirty. Some regularly donated to charity, prompted by compassion. Others became philanthropists for the sake of fame. Some were overly health-conscious or hypochondriac. Others were sensualists, frittering their lives away. Some were arrogant and self-estranged. Others were humble and amiable. Some were spiritually unconscious, intent on pleasure-seeking. Some were spiritually awake, committed to larger purposes which brought hope and strength to the less fortunate.

The paradox of life is: what we are seeking have been given to us. When we yearn for external success and recognition, what we are *really* seeking are self-acceptance and inner peace. These and much more have been given to us by our Creator when we discover the love of God. The outward storms arose and passed away. What remains is a sincere heart at rest within the oceanic Heart of God.

> *Rejoice in the Lord always. Again I will say, rejoice! Let your gentleness be known to all men ... Be anxious for nothing, but in everything by prayer and supplication, with thanksgiving, let your requests be made known to God; and the peace of God, which surpasses all understanding, will guard your hearts and minds through Christ Jesus. Philippians 4 : 4-7*

> *Attitude, to me, is more important than facts. It is more important than the past, the education, the money, than circumstances, than failure, than successes, than what other people think or say or do. It is more important than appearance, giftedness or skill. We cannot change our past ... we cannot change the fact that people will act in a certain way ... I am convinced that life is 10% what happens to me and 90% is how I respond to it.*
>
> *Dr Charles Swindoll*

We should also be vigilant against building and defending 'private' sandcastles which can hinder spiritual growth, as in the following traditional story:

A group of children was building sandcastles on a beach. After an hour each child announced that his separate sandcastle was his sole possession and would not allow others to trespass on it.

One child accidentally stepped on the sandcastle of another child. The owner was angry and shouted, "You ruined my sandcastle. I shall also destroy yours." They started to quarrel and kick at each other's sandcastles. The more mature children intervened to calm them.

When evening came and the sun began to set, the children realised that it was time to return home. They left behind their sandcastles and ran homeward.

During our journey on earth, did we forget the impermanent nature of external achievements? Did we build 'private' sandcastles to defend and declare as our sole possessions? Did we learn to let go of our sandcastles of worldly goods, sandcastles of pride and social status? Did we realize the truth of Saint Paul's words: "what is seen is temporary; what is unseen is eternal" (2 Corinthians 4:18)?

'Courage' From God

Let us share an impactful story told by Corrie Ten Boom (1892 - 1983). She is a famous Dutch Christian and a heroine. Together with her father and other family members, they helped many Jews escape the Nazis during the Second World War. I have revised and condensed her story. It enables us to remember how God has encouraged and sustained us in the past.

One morning a girl told his father that she was worried that when she encountered trials and setbacks, she might not have the strength to overcome them. Being an admirer of the courage of early Christians, she also informed her father that if she encountered a crisis, she might not have the courage to become a martyr for Jesus Christ.

The father replied, "When you need to take a train to Rome, did I provide you with the fund to buy the ticket a few months or a few weeks in advance or did I provide it on the day that you require it."

"You provided me on the day itself," said the girl.

"Thus, please do not worry. Read the Bible daily. Pray and give thanks to God daily. God will provide you with the strength and courage on a timely basis or just in time for you to handle the adversities of life."

> *Every experience God gives us, every person He puts in our lives is the perfect preparation for the future that only He can see.*
>
> *Corrie ten Boom*

The Poet Who Relied On God

One of my favourite poets is Annie Johnson Flint. For me she is a "wounded healer". She endured years of physical pain and suffering. She courageously brought back deep insights, emphasizing that reliance on God and submission to the guidance of the Holy Spirit are the only answers to our existential problems.

Annie Johnson Flint was born on Christmas Eve in 1866 in a small town in New Jersey. Her father was of

English descent while her mother was Scottish. Unfortunately her mother died in 1869 following the birth of her sister. Annie was only three years old when her mother died.

Her father brought the children to live with the widow of an old army comrade who had been killed in the Civil War. The widow had two children of her own and her means were limited. The outlook was bleak for the sisters. Fortunately Aunt Susie, a kindly neighbour, assisted them to be adopted by the Flint family. Annie's father agreed to the adoption as he was ill and he died shortly.

The new parents treated the two girls very well. They taught them to be self-reliant and thrifty. Annie learnt to make her own clothes. She was also capable of housekeeping. After finishing high school, Annie started teaching a primary class. She planned to earn regular income as Mrs Flint was failing in health. According to the contract, she was to teach for three years.

However, arthritis began to afflict her during the second year. Annie went to see several doctors, but her illness grew worse until it became difficult for her to walk. She had a very difficult time finishing her third year of teaching. After her contract ended, due to her illness, she was unable to teach and had to give up her job. Thereafter she experienced three years of increasing helplessness.

Her adopted parents passed away during this difficult period. The sisters had little money and Annie was incurring medical expenses. The faithful Aunt Susie came again to assist them. She suggested that Annie might find a cure at a sanatorium in New York. Accordingly, Annie decided to stay at the sanatorium. She rented out her house, so that she could obtain some money to care for her sister.

After examining Annie, the doctors at the sanatorium told her the disappointing news that her condition was severe. It was likely that she would continue to be an invalid. Thus, Annie's illness compelled her to be dependent on the care of others. For the rest of her life, her condition did not improve. With a pen held by bent fingers and swollen joints, she began writing poems. She also began making hand-lettered cards and gift books. Two publishers printed her cards. Nevertheless, she struggled for the rest of her life to meet her medical expenses. Although she was crippled, Annie did not consider herself useless. She believed that God had a purpose. She put her best into writing her poems, so as to encourage others. When she died in 1932, she left behind a treasury of verses which continues to inspire us in the different seasons of life. [3]

One Day at a Time

One day at a time, with its failures and fears,
With its hurts and mistakes, with its weakness and tears,
With its portion of pain and its burden of care;
One day at a time we must meet and bear.

One day at a time to be patient and strong,
To be calm under trial and sweet under wrong;
Then its toiling shall pass and its sorrow shall cease;
It shall darken and die, and the night shall bring peace.

One day at a time - but the day is so long,
And the heart is not brave, and the soul is not strong,

O merciful Christ, be Thou near all the way;
Give courage and patience and strength for the day.

Swift cometh His answer, so clear and so sweet;
"Yea, I will be with thee, thy troubles to meet;
I will not forget thee nor fail thee;
I will not forsake thee; I never will leave."

Not yesterday's load we are called on to bear,
Nor tomorrow's uncertain and shadowy care;
Why should we look forward or back with dismay?
Our needs, as our mercies, are but for the day.

One day at a time, and the day is His day;
He hath numbered its hours, though they haste or delay.
His grace is sufficient; we walk not alone;
As the day, so the strength that He giveth His own.

Annie Johnson Flint

The Best Definition of Love

The best definition of love that I came across was from Dr Wayne Dyer: "Love is the art of giving. It expects nothing in return."

Let us share a well-known real life story. Edwarda O'Bara (March 1953 – Nov 2012) was an American who spent 42 years in a diabetic coma after contracting pneumonia at the age of sixteen. Before slipping into the coma, she pleaded with her mother Kaye, "You won't leave me will you, Mom?"

Her mother Kaye responded, "I will never leave you. I promise ..."

In the next 38 years until she passed away at the age of 81 in year 2008, Kaye took care of her daughter. She fed Edwarda from a tube. She turned her daughter from side to side every few hours to prevent bedsores and changed her diaper. She gave her daughter insulin every four hours. She also read, played music and made conversation with her daughter. Her family also raised money to pay for the medical bills. After Kaye's death, Edwarda was cared for by her sister until her death in Nov 2012. [4]

The unconditional love of Kaye for her daughter has inspired thousands. Both Kaye and Edwarda contributed greatly to the moral dimension of life. Kaye was the exemplar of unconditional love and devotion, adding this priceless quality and dimension to life. On Edwarda's part, she was an appreciative recipient of love. She provided opportunities for others to show love, care and compassion for her and her family members.

Honored In Heaven

Once there was a farmer whose ten-year-old son was drowned in a nearby river. The farmer and his wife were grief-stricken. The boy was their only son. He was obedient, filial and kind-hearted. Their neighbours mourned the loss with them.

One year passed. The neighbours observed that the farmer and his wife remained sorrowful and depressed. The plot of land owned by the farmer was uncultivated during that year.

The neighbours explained the situation to three elderly teachers and invited them to console the farmer and his wife. The three wisdom teachers agreed and they went to the farmer's house one morning. They consoled the couple and mourned the loss with them for seven days.

On the eighth day, the teachers began to play gentle music with their flutes. The farmer became angry and enquired why they were playing music.

"Please do not be angry," explained one of the teachers gently. "Please realise that the soul of your son has gone to heaven. He is now enjoying eternal joy and harmony. We have finite minds. We do not know why God decided to bring your son back to His kingdom. We could not see His long-term plan. But we can hold on to our faith that what God has decided for us is for our eternal best. We learn to accept that God will decide whether we live one day more or less. We know that when it is time for us to leave this world, we will be reunited with your son in heaven."

"Please also realise that the children of your neighbours are also your children," said another teacher. "We are all children of God. If we expand our perspective, we can regard other people's children as our children. You can better appreciate the abilities of these children and the joy they bring to the world. You can also visit the orphanage in the village and consider to regard some of the orphans as your children. Perhaps please consider to contribute a portion of your income to them. They will be very grateful to you."

"Yes, it is helpful to discover our real identities that we are all children of God," said the third teacher. "When our journey on earth ends, our souls will return to the kingdom of God. Thus, please rise above the mental labels of "your children" and "my children". Please discover the immortal essence within us. Please rise above the mental labels of "yours" and "mine", "gains" and "losses". This is the route to genuine peace and faith in God. We can thereby serve God until He decides to bring us home."

The farmer and his wife thanked the teachers for their advice. The next day they began to grow vegetables and fruits on their land. They also visited the orphanage in the village and adopted two orphans as their children. They also contributed a quarter of their annual income to the orphanage for thirty years before they retired.

When they died of old age and went to heaven, the angels greeted them. They were joyful to see their son. They were also surprised to see a statue erected in heaven to commend their generous contributions to the orphanage. The angels explained to them that their kind deeds might not be recognised by others on earth, but their generosity was all along recognised by God. In addition, their contributions to the orphanage enabled a significant number of the orphans to attend schools in the city who became useful citizens to the country. [5]

"My Grace Is Sufficient For You ..."

> *For I am convinced that neither death nor life, neither angels nor demons, neither the present nor the future, nor any powers, neither height nor depth, nor anything else in all creation, will be able to separate us from the love of God that is in Christ Jesus our Lord.*
>
> *Romans 8 : 38 - 39*

What God Has Promised

God has not promised skies always blue,
Flower-strewn pathways all through our lives;
God has not promised the sun without rain,

Joy without sorrow, peace without pain.

God has not promised we shall not know
Toil and temptation, trouble and woe;
He has not told us we shall not bear
Many a burden, many a care.

But God has promised strength for the day,
Rest for the laborer, light for the way,
Grace for the trials, help from above,
Unfailing sympathy, undying love.
Annie Johnson Flint

May I share the following real life stories which have inspired me over the years.

"Miraculous Joe" : In Dr Gerald Jampolsky's bestselling book *Love Is Letting Go Of Fear*, he related a real life story about Joe, a fifteen-year-old boy whose head had been run over twice by a tractor. While at the hospital, the doctors discovered that the accident had rendered him blind, mute and sensationless. Joe was in a coma for months. The doctors were not hopeful that he would survive.

However, Joe's family did not give up hope. They prayed and lived one day at a time. A series of miracles began to happen. Joe recovered consciousness. Gradually he recovered his ability to speak. Slowly he began to walk. Joe's positive spirit and attitude astonished everyone, including Dr Jampolsky. When Joe became better, although he was still blind, he began to talk to other patients and encouraged them.

When Dr Jampolsky asked Joe how he could remain so positive and helpful, he replied, "I just look at the positive things in everyone and pay no attention to the negative things and refuse to believe in the word *impossible.*" [6] By extending kind thoughts to others, Joe manifested the love of the Holy Spirit flowing through him.

"Miraculous Minister of Hope": Mr Don Piper is often being introduced as the Minister of Hope. He is the bestselling author of *Ninety Minutes in Heaven.*

In his book he explained that on 18 January 1989, he died in an automobile accident. He emphasized that it was not a near-death experience. Two EMTs pronounced him dead and he spent ninety minutes in heaven before a pastor prayed him back to earth.

After the accident, he had to undergo thirty-four surgeries. Because of his heavenly experiences and the deep pain and suffering he had endured due to the accident, he was able to share his experiences with others and encouraged them. These are his memorable words, "Wonderful, loving God, help me fill my mind with the best and the purest thoughts. Help me keep my attention on you during the worst situations and you will give me your deep inner tranquillity. You will take me through all the difficult times and I am grateful." [7]

*"**Miraculous Faith**"*: In his bestselling book *It's Not About Me,* Mr Max Lucado was visiting his friend in a hospital who had cancer. His friend had prayed many times to God to heal his sickness. But nothing seemed to happen. His cancer remained. He was confused, perplexed and on the verge of despair.

Max Lucado suggested another response, "It's not about you. Your hospital room is a showcase for your

Maker. Your faith in the face of suffering cranks up the volume of God's song."

His friend's face brightened up. He realised that he had not failed God and God had not failed him. There was a deeper purpose in his suffering and afflictions. He had a choice. He could choose to see his sickness in terms of God's eternal purpose. Gradually he rediscovered his faith. He rediscovered his sense of dignity and purpose in the midst of suffering. He learnt to accept his cancer as an assignment from God. He chose to become a missionary in the cancer ward. He made a commitment to reflect faith in God, by displaying courageous smiles to all, to the nurses, to the doctors, to all his friends. He told Max Lucado, "Who knows who needed to see God, but I did my best to make Him seen ..." [8]

"Miraculous Nick Vujicic": Nick was born in 1982 in Melbourne, Australia. He was born with severe disabilities. He has no arms and no legs. Thousands have watched his You Tube video showing how he went through his daily life. For all of us with arms and legs, suddenly we felt very fortunate and blessed. Imagine having no arms and no legs. How do we survive, let alone finding a job?

In his bestselling book *Life Without Limits*, Nick described his confusion, sadness and struggles as an adolescent with issues of self-esteem and self-image. During his dark moments at a young age, he was planning a suicide so that he would not be a burden to others. At the critical moment, Nick realised that he could not bear the thought of leaving his beloved parents behind. His father's subsequent words also encouraged him, "We will always be here for you."

Nick has since become a best-selling author and the CEO of a non-profit organisation. He travelled around the world, speaking to millions of people and in church congregations of all sizes. He wrote, "I realised that my purpose was to turn my struggles into lessons that glorify God and inspire others. He blessed me as a blessing to others. Distribute your own blessings with enthusiasm, and know that whatever you do will be multiplied many times. In all things God works for the best for those who love Him."

In Nick's book, he also narrated a real life story about a twenty-year-old woman who lived in India. She was kidnapped from her rural home at the age of ten and was forced to become a prostitute in the streets of Bombay. By the time she was thirteen she managed to clear her 'debts' owed to the operators of the brothel. However, when she reached home, her family did not want her. Without a home, she was again forced to work as a prostitute in the streets of Bombay. Recently she discovered that she contracted AIDS and her pimp fired her. Thus she became homeless. Fortunately she was given shelter and medical treatment by a Christian agency where she heard about Jesus. The missionaries were deeply moved by her misfortune. She found spiritual strength after she learnt about the gospel. With astonishing hope in God, she told the missionaries, "Now I know God did not cure me of AIDS because I could bring other women to Christ." [9]

Her response reminded me of the words of Viktor Frankl, the author of the classic *Man's Search For Meaning*. He was imprisoned at Auschwitz and other concentration camps for three years during the Second World War. Although I read his great book several times in the past fifteen years, I could now more fully appreciate the depth of his insights into the meaning of suffering: "When a man finds that it is his destiny to suffer, he will have to accept his suffering as his task: his single and unique task ... His unique opportunity lies in the way in which he bears his burden. For us the meaning of life embraced the wider cycles of life and death, of suffering and dying. There was no need to be ashamed of tears, for tears bore witness that a man had the greatest of courage, the courage to suffer."

"Miraculous Saint Maximilian Kolbe": Saint Maximilian Kolbe was born in Russian-occupied Poland in 1894. His parents initially worked as basket weavers. Later his mother operated a shop selling groceries. His life was strongly influenced by a childhood vision of the Virgin Mary which he later described: "That night, I asked the Mother of God what was to become of me, a child of Faith. Then she came to me holding two crowns, one white, the other red. She asked me if I was willing to accept either of these crowns. The white one meant that I should persevere in purity and the red one meant that I should become a martyr. I said that I would accept them both."

In 1914, Kolbe took his final vows. He studied and earned a doctorate in philosophy in 1915 and a doctorate in theology in 1919. He was ordained a priest before he returned to Poland.

After the outbreak of the Second World War, Father Kolbe's monastery became a refugee camp for thousands of Poles and Jews who were seeking to escape from Nazi persecution. As a publisher who had refused German citizenship, Father Kolbe was considered a threat to the Germans. To incriminate him, the Gestapo permitted one final printing of the "Knight of Mary Immaculate" in Dec 1940. It was in this issue that Father Kolbe wrote:

> *No one in the world can change Truth. What we can do and should do is to seek Truth and to serve it when we have found it. The real conflict is inner conflict. Beyond armies of occupation and the catacombs of concentration camps, there are two irreconcilable enemies in the depth of every soul: good and evil, sin and love. And what use are victories on the battle-field if we ourselves are defeated in our innermost personal selves?*

In February 1941 he was arrested by the Germans. Soon he was transferred to Auschwitz as a prisoner. He was put to hard labor. In July 1941 three prisoners disappeared from the camp. The deputy camp commander selected ten men to be starved to death to deter escape attempts. When one of the selected men cried out, "My wife! My children!", Father Kolbe volunteered to take his place.

In his prison cell, Father Kolbe encouraged the condemned men with songs and prayers. After two weeks of starvation, only Father Kolbe remained alive. The guards injected him with lethal carbolic acid. Some who were present said that Father Kolbe raised his left arm calmly and waited for the injection. He was canonized in 1982 as a Martyr of Charity. [10]

Equally immortal are the deeds and words of Saint Paul. He was imprisoned many times for spreading the gospel. He was flogged by the Jews, beaten with rods, stoned once and shipwrecked three times. He had to labour and toil and he had often gone without food. He also suffered from a thorn in his flesh and pleaded with God to take it away. But God said, “My grace is sufficient for you, for my power is made perfect in weakness.”

Saint Paul said that for Christ's sake, he delighted in weaknesses, in insults and hardships, in persecutions and difficulties. For when he felt physically weak, he remained spiritually strong by relying on God, the eternal Strength and Stronghold.

Serving God's Purposes

May we remember that a single lamp can light our path. A single sunbeam can clear the doubts. A single inspiration can bring deep awakening. A kind-hearted deed can change the direction of a person's life. The steadfast love, faith and hope of our spiritual ancestors manifested the true messages of the perennial wisdom and charted the long-term course of human civilization.

May we realise the astonishing insight of Saint Paul who observed that the treasures of light and strength that shine within us are held in perishable containers, in our weak bodies, in jars of clay, so that everyone can see that our glorious strength comes from God and not from our weak bodies (2 Corinthians 4:7).

May we remind ourselves every day of Saint Paul's insight that although we may feel physically weak, God is forever strong. There is eternal hope and strength in our Creator as reflected in the well-known twenty-third Psalm :

The Lord is my shepherd, I shall not be in want.

He makes me lie down in green pastures, he leads me beside quiet waters, he restores my soul.

He guides me in paths of righteousness for his name's sake.

Even though I walk through the valley of the shadow of death, I will fear no evil, for you are with me; your rod and your staff, they comfort me.

You prepare a table before me in the presence of my enemies. You anoint my head with oil; my cup overflows.

Surely goodness and unfailing love will follow me all the days of my life, and I will dwell in the house of the Lord forever.

May we pray the prayer of Saint Francis every day and give thanks to God for His sustenance, guidance, strength and love.

May we share Saint Paul's insight that neither height nor depth, nor anything else in all creation, can separate us from the love of God.

May we realise that to give is to receive, to forgive others is to be released from hatred.

May we realise that God does not want us to bear the cross unless it reveals the eternal life within us, unless it is for our eternal best, unless it contributes to the moral dimension of life.

May we realise that our inner essence is always wholesome, pure and intact. May we realise that we will return to the kingdom of God when our journey on earth ends.

May we listen to the voice of our soul every day, extend a helping hand to the needy and do something beautiful for God. In this way we are serving God's purposes in our generation.

Nothing that is worth doing can be achieved in our lifetime; therefore we must be saved by hope.

Nothing which is true or beautiful or good makes complete sense in the immediate context of history; therefore we must be saved by faith.

Reinhold Niebuhr

On earth we have nothing to do with success or results, but only with being true to God. Defeat in doing right is nevertheless victory.

Frederick Robertson

Every spiritual life entails a succession of difficulties because every ordinary life also involves a succession of difficulties ... In a spiritually informed life, however, these inevitable difficulties can be the source of our awakening, of deepening wisdom, patience, balance and compassion.

Dr Jack Kornfield

If there is anywhere on earth a lover of God who is always kept safe, I know nothing of it, for it was not shown to me. But this was shown: that in falling and rising again, we are always kept in that same precious love.

An Autumn of Faith

(Sharing His Messages of Faith, Understanding and Inner Peace)

Autumn

All day I have watched the purple vine leaves
Fall into the water.
And now in the moonlight they still fall,
But each leaf is fringed with silver.

Amy Lowell

For in Him we live and move and have our being. As some of your own poets have said, 'We are His offspring.'

Acts 17 : 28

Man has not invented God.
He has developed faith,
To meet a God already there.

Edna St. Vincent Millay

The Twins

A pair of twins had stayed in their mother's womb for eight months. One of them was known as the Ego. The other was known as the Spirit.

"Brother, do you think we will be born into a world filled with light?" asked the Spirit one morning.

"What kind of world are you talking about? We only have this world which is dark," said the Ego.

"Last night I had a vision," explained the Spirit. "It revealed to me that we will be born into a world filled with light. I believe in it."

"Do not engage in useless speculation. Try to get used to this dark watery world. We will be fine," said the Ego.

The Spirit said, "I sense that there is a divine Intelligence coursing through our bodies. This divine Intelligence is patiently guiding the development of our cells. It is guiding the growth of our tissues, organs and bodily systems, such as our beating hearts, lungs, brain cells, hands and feet. It is guiding the growth of our digestive system, immune system, nervous system and skeletal system. I sense that this Intelligence wants us to know Him and to follow Him after we are born."

"If you wish to indulge in groundless chatters, please continue," said the Ego. "For me there is only this dark watery world."

Two months later, the twins felt prolonged movements in the womb. They soon found themselves being pushed by the muscles through the narrow passage of the womb and into a world of light. [1]

Pointing To The Truth

Once there was a young man who travelled for five days from his hometown to reach a village where a well-known teacher stayed.

Upon reaching the village, he asked for direction to the teacher's hut. When he saw the old teacher, he bowed and introduced himself, explaining that he wished to seek wisdom. When he was inside the hut where the teacher was teaching his ten students, he noticed that the teacher only had one book and some furniture.

The young man asked the teacher, "Master, where is your treasury of books? I thought you are a well-read man with comprehensive knowledge on many subjects."

"I teach simplicity," replied the old teacher. "May I enquire where are your books?"

"I did not bring them," said the young man in surprise. "I am only visiting you and passing by."

The teacher replied, "So am I. We are all visitors on earth."

The young man felt that the teacher was not able to impart useful knowledge to him and he left.

One of the students in the hut commented, "What a pity. Due to his preconception about the importance of book knowledge, he missed the opportunity to learn from you."

"His journey towards Reality has begun," said the teacher. "It is a matter of time. Once his spirit is kindled, there is no turning back. We are surrounded by Reality, by the Truth. The books only point to the Truth." [2]

My home is in Heaven. I'm just travelling through this world.

Dr Billy Graham

The Interconnected Nature of Life

The most beautiful and profound emotion we can experience is the sensation of the mystical. *Albert Einstein*

To awaken to God's gifts of inner peace, we can read a devotional book, listen to inspiring music or visit the seaside, so that our awareness is expanded. This can prompt us to appreciate the beauty of nature and the creative power of God. It can also make us appreciate the interconnected nature of life. For example, please reflect on the book which you are now reading. Its interconnected nature is reflected in William Blake's poem:

To see a world in a grain of sand
And a heaven in a wild flower,
Hold infinity in the palm of your hand
And eternity in an hour.

This poem implies that a small thing can contain universal truths if we have the right perspective. It implies that a grain of sand reflects the miracle of existence. It prompts you to ponder: Why is there *something* rather than *nothing*? To go deeper, a wild flower reflects the miracle of life. We can ponder: Why does *life* exist? Why does *consciousness* exist rather than *nothingness*?

The poem also implies the interconnected nature of life. For example, this book came from the efforts of many people --- the logger sawing down the tree, the driver transporting the timber to the factory, the factory workers and technicians processing the timber into paper-making materials, the scientists specializing in paper-making technology, the publishing managers overseeing its design and printing and so forth.

Further, it came into existence because the tree from which it originated was nourished by energy from the sun, nutrients from the soil and rainwater from the sky. Hence, the preconditions of its existence included solar energy, soil, rainwater, the natural processes of photosynthesis, planet Earth and the sun. In turn, the existence of planet Earth and the sun depended on the existence of the Milky Way and the Milky Way in turn was connected with other galaxies. Thus, from this perspective, this book subtly and miraculously mirrors the existence of the cosmos.

Study the art of science. Study the science of art. Use and develop all your senses, especially your sense of vision. In the light of all knowledge, remember that everything connects, in some way or another, to everything else.

Leonardo Da Vinci

Meditation And Finding Our Real Identity

Very early in the morning, while it was still dark, Jesus got up, left the house and went off to a solitary place where he prayed.

Mark 1:35

Let the words of my mouth and the meditation of my heart be acceptable in Your sight, O LORD, my strength and my Redeemer.

Psalm 19 : 14

Meditation is one way to awaken to God's gift of inner peace. Years of meditation have deepened my insights into Psalm 46:10 “Be still and know that I am God.”

Usually in the evening I sat alone in a quiet place. I closed my eyes and meditated. I learned to become physically and mentally still. I learned to watch my in-breaths and out-breaths, and witness the arising and passing away of my thoughts, feelings and desires. I learned not to chase after them.

There is no competition and no failure in meditation. If I felt frustrated, sad or anxious, these feelings and the thoughts giving rise to these feelings are the ‘contents’ to let go during meditation. In quietly watching or counting my in-breaths and out-breaths, if I were distracted by intruding thoughts or feelings, I gently let them go. I learned to restart the process and patiently waited for the serenity within to surface. I sought to become familiar with the workings of the hyperactive mind.

In becoming familiar with the workings of the mind and its hyperactive energies, I learned to befriend them. They were useful during our ordinary waking consciousness. They were harnessed to reason, analyse and solve practical problems. During meditation, I learned to let go of these hyperactive energies. I let the thoughts and feelings to arise and pass away, without chasing them. Slowly the 'pure consciousness' within surfaced. It was like a miniature cosmos. It was like a hologram of the cosmos which mirrored the beautiful night sky. This 'pure consciousness' is the fourth state of consciousness that meditation teachers frequently talked about. The other three states refer to our ordinary waking consciousness, our dreaming state and the state of deep sleep.

Slowly I realised that there is no substantial "I". Our thoughts, feelings and desires are momentary. They are flashes of mental energies. They arise and pass away. They do not construct a permanent "I", "me" or "myself". They do not construct our personality. They are not our real identity. It is our thinking habits and patterns which seek to create a 'selfhood' or 'personality' out of these flashes of energies.

For Christians, meditation is a useful tool that can deepen our awareness and understanding that 'pure consciousness' is a key attribute of our 'soul'. If we meditate regularly, we realize that 'pure consciousness' is a portal for catching glimpses of God's presence. Slowly we realize that our soul is always wholesome and intact. It is eternal. Nothing can affect it. Nothing can impair it. It comes from our Creator. It is His priceless gift to us. This realization will deepen our faith. This will deepen our awareness that we are always connected to the love of a living God. As our habit of meditation stabilises over the years, we realise that part of the tranquillity we experienced during meditation can flow to our ordinary waking consciousness. This enables us to be more calm, conscientious and patient in our daily lives.

Letting Go of "Inner War"

> *The true value of a human being is determined primarily by the measure and the sense in which he has attained liberation from the self.*
>
> *Albert Einstein*

Discovering our real identity is essential to stopping the 'inner war'. We realise that 'ego' is not a physical entity. It is not our 'personality'. It is not our 'selfhood'. It is made up of self-seeking energies, thoughts and desires. These are flashes of mental energies. They arise and pass away.

This insight is crucial. If we do not understand that the ego is only made up of fleeting mental energies, we can misconceive that it is our personality or selfhood. We can become trapped by such erroneous thinking. We can become imprisoned by 'inner psychological war' which we wage subconsciously with our siblings, neighbours, colleagues, friends and relatives when we seek to protect our pride and sense of self-importance. It is a vicious cycle. We seek external success to protect our sense of self-importance. When we attain it, we fear to lose it and we continue to chase for greater external success.

When we meditate, we become aware of this vicious cycle. We become aware of unhealthy mental states that arise from self-seeking energies. They include anxiety, frustration, greed, anger and discontent. During meditation, we learn to watch the arising and passing away of these mental energies. We become more familiar with their transitory nature. They lose their grip on us.

In addition, in catching glimpses of our soul and its attribute of pure consciousness, we realize the priceless gifts of God within us. We realize that we are always connected to the love of a living God. Inwardly we are always receiving His gifts of love, compassion, strength and courage. This enables us to experience inner peace. Slowly we realize that God is sufficient for our needs. God will take care of our eternal best. In this way we learn to let go of 'egoistic' motives. We learn to let go of 'inner war'.

> *Whatever selfishness is in our minds, whatever unkindness or insensitivity to other creatures is in our life, is all merely a covering. It is just a thick layer of conditioning that hides our real goodness and kindness.*
>
> *Eknath Easwaran*

> *Your ego is a set of thoughts that define your universe. It's like a familiar room built of thoughts. You are secure in it, but to the extent that you are afraid to venture outside, it has become a prison.*
>
> *Ram Dass*

Once there were four young rivers flowing down a green mountain. They called the mountain their earthly mother. They called the great winds their earthly father.

As they flowed down the mountain, the sibling rivers played with each other, enjoying each other's company. They were filled with affection for each other.

Soon they reached the bottom of the mountain. They began to flow over the green hills and into the plains and farmlands. They were praised by the farmers and the villagers for meeting their daily needs. Slowly the four rivers became proud.

The First River acquired a sense of self-importance and claimed that he was most important as he brought the most amount of water to the villagers.

The Second River disagreed and claimed that he should be the center of praise as he was nearer to the houses of the villagers and that they used his water more frequently.

The Third River disagreed and claimed that the farmers used his water more often for irrigation and for washing their farming tools.

The Fourth River disagreed and claimed that his water contained a larger number and variety of fish and that the villagers fished in his water more often.

Thus the four rivers kept quarrelling with each other. The mountain and the great winds intervened and sought to explain to them their real essence and their Source. However, the four rivers did not pay attention.

After quarrelling for the whole morning and ignoring the explanations of the mountain and the winds, the four rivers saw sparkles in the distance. Slowly they saw the vastness of the blue Ocean. Gradually they realised their real identity and their Source.

The sibling rivers calmed down and reconciled. They realised that the credit rightfully belonged to the Ocean. They were channels of the Ocean bringing her gifts to the farmers and villagers. With gratitude they flowed into and merged with the Ocean of life. [3]

Is It Day time or Night time?

Let us share a traditional wisdom tale which I have revised.

A group of truth-seekers visited an elderly teacher for advice.

The teacher enquired how they knew the difference between night time and the coming of dawn.

Some seekers suggested that when they looked into the distance and saw a tree and they could tell whether it was a fig tree and a peach tree, this would indicate the coming of dawn. Others suggested that when they looked into the distance and saw an animal and they could tell whether it was a sheep or a cow.

The teacher explained, "When we look into the face of every man and woman and realise that they are our brothers and sisters, then dawn has arrived and daytime has come. Otherwise it is night time."

The seekers agreed and asked, "How do we reach that kind of realisation?"

"At this moment, is it night time or daytime in your mental universe?" asked the teacher.

"We do not understand. Please explain to us," said the seekers.

"When our minds are filled with self-seeking thoughts, when we regard others as rivals, when we are filled with anxiety, fear and envy, can we perceive others as our brothers and sisters?" asked the teacher. "If this is our mental state, if this is our mental universe, it is night time."

"How do we change it to daytime?" asked the seekers.

"Please discover your real identity. Discover your spiritual essence and the unconditional love of our Creator. These are the priceless gifts from God," said the teacher. "When we realise that the priceless gifts within are always there and cannot be taken away, we are freed from anxiety, fear and envy. We are freed from self-imposed rivalry. We are freed from the prison of self-seeking thoughts. When we cultivate compassion, we begin to see others as friends, as brothers and sisters. This is the beginning of daytime."

The group of seekers agreed.

The elderly teacher continued, "Please realise that there is no permanent night time in our mental universe. During those moments when we experienced sympathy and big-hearted compassion, we experienced moments of day time. During other moments when our hearts were closed, when we experienced anger and discontent, there would be night time. Thus, please cultivate big-hearted compassion so that we can experience day time more often ..." [4]

Broad Empiricism

> *Mystery is not the absence of meaning, but the presence of more meaning than we can comprehend.*
>
> *Dennis Covington*

> *I have observed the power of the watermelon seed. It has the power of drawing from the ground and through itself 200,000 times its weight. When you can tell me how it takes this material and out of it colors an outside surface beyond the imitation of art, and then forms inside of it a white rind and within that again a red heart, thickly inlaid with*

black seeds, each one of which in turn is capable of drawing through itself 200,000 times its weight --- when you can explain to me the mystery of a watermelon, you can ask me to explain the mystery of God.

William Jennings Bryan

Many of us may hold the view that 'pure consciousness' is brain-based and that it does not have independent existence. In my early years as a Christian, I also harboured this thought. After many years of meditation and reading Christian, New Age and contemporary science literature, I discovered that more scientists are beginning to accept that there is a difference between 'consciousness' and the brain.

For example, many scientists are baffled as to how do we have memories of events that are more than ten, twenty or thirty years old, when all our brain cells and neural networks are changing and renewing all the time in the past ten, twenty or thirty years. To propose that our memories are stored in fluid memory centres in various parts of the brain is akin to saying that memory is stored in water.

In addition, modern scientists agree that the brain cells, neurones and all our bodily cells and organs are made of atoms and molecules which are 99.99 percent empty. They are only vibrating energies. They are not solid entities. Thus there is no genuine material substratum in the first place.

Western materialistic sciences have not solved the mystery regarding the gap between matter and consciousness. They have not solved the origin and nature of human consciousness and higher states of awareness. Generally, if something cannot be measured or detected by scientific instruments, it does not fall within the ambit of scientific studies. Many philosophers consider this to be 'narrow empiricism'. This approach will give rise to a reductionist 'flatland' conception of the universe. Based on this 'narrow empiricism' model, many Western neuroscientists hold that human consciousness and higher states of awareness are generated by neuro-physiological processes in the brain. It is based on their belief in the primacy of matter in the universe.

Nevertheless there is another group of scientists and psychologists who support 'broad empiricism'. They are open to consider subjective human experiences as another type of empirical data. They believe that there are many important data showing that human consciousness can exist and function independently of the body and of the physical senses. These evidential data were accumulated from researches relating to parapsychology, anthropology, experiential psychotherapy and studies of non-ordinary states of consciousness. They are moving in the direction that 'Consciousness' or energy and information are the primary elements driving the creation and evolution of this universe.

Developmental Psychologists have proposed stages of mental growth. During its first year, the infant develops its capacity for sensation and perception. Between the ages of one and three, the baby develops its capacity for impulses and emotions and its ability for thinking in images. From the age of three to six, the child begins to develop its mental ability to understand symbols and concepts that will form the basis for language learning and reading. From age seven onwards, the child learns to perform rule-based tasks and acquires practical knowledge. From age twelve onwards till early adult stage, the child will develop its ability for more complex rational thinking, deductive analysis and reasoning, and will learn how to develop socially acceptable behaviour.

In addition, transpersonal psychologists are of the view that human beings can develop beyond this 'rational understanding' stage and expand their ordinary states of consciousness to reach higher states of consciousness. We are not regressing to pre-rational childish innocence. We are moving towards a trans-conceptual stage where we gradually understand the limits of conceptual language and conceptual understanding. This is the pre /trans fallacy as highlighted by a growing number of wisdom teachers and philosophers who are supportive of moving towards higher trans-conceptual states of awareness in the spiritual evolution of humankind. To quote Einstein, many conceptual problems cannot be resolved at the mental-conceptual levels. Depending on the nature of the problems, creative approaches at the trans-conceptual level are useful.

On my part, I agree with this 'broad empiricism' approach. After many years of studies and meditative experiences, I realise that higher states of consciousness like long-term intention, will power, moral determination and spiritual qualities such as compassion, courage and the spirit of self-sacrifice do not originate from the brain. They come from the 'soul'.

For example, if we went for a picnic at the park and a wolf suddenly appeared and postured itself to attack our young child, most of us would rush forward to protect our child, regardless of the danger that we might be bitten or killed. This 'courage' does not originate from the brain. When we saw this event, the visual, perceptual and reflective stimuli would trigger our brain cells and body organs for a fight or flight response, not to protect the child, but to protect ourselves. Self-preservation is the first evolutionary priority of the brain. The 'courage', 'moral strength and willpower', and the 'spirit of self-sacrifice' to protect our child come from the 'soul'. From this perspective, when combined with the physical body, the embodied soul need to awaken in its life journey so as to become mature and manifest spiritual qualities. If the embodied soul is not mature, it is not able to overcome the fear of bodily injury and death.

A Responsible-To-God Approach To Spiritual Growth

One night a wisdom-seeker dreamed that he met God while walking along the beach. He enquired, "How do I know that my life is moving in the right direction?"

God replied, "You are moving in the right direction when you listen to your conscience every day. You release selfish desires. You choose simplicity. You rise above the need to impress others. You entrust yourself, your future and your loved ones to Me. You uphold the belief that My decisions are for your eternal best. You experience inner peace more often. These are the key indicators."

The seeker said, "Thank you, God. How do I practice forgiveness?"

God replied, "Remind yourself daily that people around you behave according to their level of spiritual and moral awareness. If they have a low level of such awareness, they tend to display selfish behaviour. Please pray that they awaken soon.

“In practising forgiveness, it does not mean that you agree with immoral and wrongful deeds. Do continue to voice your objections to immoral and wrongful deeds that harm people. But inwardly, you learn to forgive others for their lack of spiritual awareness, particularly if they are repentant.

“Forgiving others also does not mean that you allow immature people to emotionally or physically abuse you. Please value and care for yourself in a wise way. You are My precious child, My vessel of love. If despite your objections and advice, those immature people continue to abuse, hurt or mistreat you, please leave the situation. Find a suitable place and environment where you can learn useful skills and knowledge, so that you can find a job or engage in meaningful activities that contribute to your well-being and the well-being of others. Your job or activities should also develop your qualities of wisdom, compassion, inner balance, simplicity, faith and inner peace.

“Further, when you perform a kind deed, do not expect others to be grateful. Their level of gratitude depends on their level of spiritual awareness. Be assured that I am aware of your kind deeds. Please also realise that you can slip into spiritual non-awareness every now and then. Always be attentive and vigilant against selfish thoughts."

The seeker said, "Thank you, God."

God said, "Please also reflect whether your daily thoughts, choices, words and deeds are healthy or unhealthy. 'Healthy' means 'conducive to your physical, mental and spiritual well-being'. It is conducive to developing qualities like wisdom, compassion, humility, patience, faith and selfless service. 'Unhealthy' means 'strengthening self-seeking energies'. To conclude, when you are conscientious and kind, when you choose to be responsible to Me and engage in thoughts, words or deeds that contribute to the well-being of others, you are moving in the right direction."

The seeker said, "May I enquire what are the secrets to happiness?"

God replied, "First, please realise that you can enjoy the beauty of nature without competing with others. This is genuine abundance. When you feel sad, please visit the beach. Let the sea breezes, the blue sky, the warm sunshine, and the rhythms of the waves comfort your soul and heal your body.

"Second, release the attachments in your mind. Please realise that you can enjoy the beauty of nature without competing with others. People who are competing for material goods have not found the true treasures of life. Attachments to external success hinder spiritual growth. Resistance to external losses hinders growth. Please let go and release them. What is most precious and valuable to you cannot be taken away from you. It is always within you. My love for you is always within you. You are always connected to My love, peace, understanding and unseen abundance.

"Third, simplify your life. Do not seek to collect and hoard material things. Simplify. Be frugal. Be considerate. Be compassionate. Share with the needy. Pray daily. Follow Me faithfully. Simplicity is abundance."

Those Daily Seasons [5]

Morning walks bring common yet uncommon scenes,
suggesting the dawn of *life*,
miracles that do not leave us
if we find that spot:
where everything quiets down,
waiting, longing for the *awareness* to grow,
a *knowing* to surface,
where once again, we become light and thin,
ready to blend with deep green foliage,
ready to become a gleam in the eyes of a squirrel,
or become a sparkle of sunlight
on the surface of a lotus pond;
or perhaps merge with some of the rays
shedding light on His footprints along the path,
or even changed by His whispers
into the voice of a stream.
Such mystical blessings of a Spring within us;
the *awareness* knows where to find them
since it has never been separated from them ...

Back home, the noontime warmth of the rays
seems to dispel some of the mystery of dawn,
as if Summer is nudging us to fulfil a mission

with grace, truth and courage --
but until I learn to trust,
to rely on the Greater Power and Goodness;
an awakening I receive from that hybrid *koi*
spots of white, red and orange,
swimming in that kind of Grace,
in a garden pool,
a *simplicity* yet complex in its every motion,
every glide and quickening,
every turn and tilt --
it enlivens *life* and all things around me,
as if saying: "Please look behind ..."
Suddenly I realize
the *koi,* me and us
are all along being witnessed
and sustained from behind
by all-knowing Eyes ...

Evening arrives with Autumn coolness;
it brings an unexpected guest:
a wide-eyed moth hunting, pursuing, chasing
a flame housed within a festive lantern.
Although relentless as the flame,

it cannot enter the narrow opening;
its wings are saved from being burned.
But its movements seem to resent me
for interfering with its wish
of becoming a martyred beauty,
perhaps a kind of union with the Unseen,
to make me feel bowels-deep
how courageous is the Source,
making the Word to become flesh,
a *Tenderness* exposed,
whispering those secrets of the ages:
"Without death,
can there be breathing *aliveness*?
Without death,
can there be *Deeds* of selfless sacrifice,
the finest *Treasures* of the cosmos?"
But God, being wiser, goes further:
death is only a cosmic veil,
behind it is Eternal life ...

The cool night air accompanies our meditative rest,
bringing ordinary yet beyond-ordinary quietness,
as if the world can be seen, felt, heard, created anew,

always for the first time,
a mystery as deep as a clear night sky.

The hyperactive mind can travel far and wide,
even touching the starlight
which appears to retell ancient Winter tales
of some far-away galaxies.

Or the mind can travel to the past,
to those faraway forests and hills,
where battles had been fought,
filled with turmoil, fires, smoke and ashes ...
until slowly it settles down to inner healing,
within that mist of forest quiet,
within half-hidden streams.
The *silence* within surfaces
where time fades away.

Perhaps someday we may even experience
how a grateful *spirit* can be born
from the depth of that *silence*:
an ancient *silence*
willing to share some of its Mysteries

whereby the meek will inherit a new earth,
the peacemakers will become His children,
the pure in heart will sense His presence,
the faithful will finally dwell in His house,
the Truth will make us free.

Perhaps we may even be allowed
to catch a glimpse:
where the same grateful *spirit*
travels across the wide seas and ocean beds,
carried by their mystery to the heart
of riverbanks, pines and cedars,
to life-changing vantage points
of mountain ridges and peaks,
where beyond the mists and clouds,
its eyes finally reflect
a gleam of ongoing *revelations.*

Merton Lee

A Winter of Wisdom

(Sharing His Messages on Life's Mysteries, Problems and Wisdom)

Winter Heavens

Sharp is the night, but stars with frost alive
Leap off the rim of earth across the dome.
It is a night to make the heavens our home
More than the nest whereto apace we strive.
Lengths down our road each fir-tree seems a hive,
In swarms outrushing from the golden comb.
They waken waves of thoughts that burst to foam:
The living throb in me, the dead revive.
Yon mantle clothes us: there, past mortal breath,
Life glistens on the river of the death.
It folds us, flesh and dust; and have we knelt,
Or never knelt, or eyed as kine the springs
Of radiance, the radiance enrings:
And this is the soul's haven to have felt.

George Meredith

God has made everything beautiful in its time. He has also planted eternity in the hearts of men.

Ecclesiastes 3:11

... a time is coming and has now come when the true worshippers will worship the Father in spirit and truth, for they are the kind of worshippers the Father seeks. God is spirit, and his worshipers must worship in spirit and in truth.

John 4 : 23-24

[Merton Lee]: Thank you, God, for allowing me to experience deep insights when I meditated in the past one year. I am very grateful for Your guidance. I know that You are the Creator God. Please explain the meaning of my experiences.

God: I am that I am. I am the nameless One. I am the eternal One. I am the divine Source. I am your Creator God. I have decided to provide deep insights and revelations to you so as to explain life's mysteries. Please share them with others.

[Q] Thank you, God. Am I your messenger? Please explain.

God: Yes, you are My messenger. You will be guided by the Holy Spirit.

[Q] Please advise whether there are other messengers? How do I share Your messages with others?

God : In writing and publishing this book, you are doing fine in sharing them. The moment another person reads it, that person will also become My messenger. The sharing is done by patiently informing others of its existence and encouraging them to read it.

Please patiently inform your Christian friends, pastors, preachers, teachers and other religious believers and non-believers about this book. It is essential for them to read it. It provides valuable insights which enhance their spiritual growth. It enables believers to defend their faith. Please do not compel anyone to read it. Patiently inform your friends. That is sufficient. They will be guided sooner or later by the Holy Spirit to read it.

[Q] Please explain why the year 2012 is chosen.

God: I have made this important decision. Many virtuous, kind-hearted, compassionate and courageous human beings had over many generations greatly contributed to the moral dimension of life in the visible world. They had contributed, endured, suffered and sacrificed without full understanding of My ultimate purpose in creating the visible world. They had contributed, endured, suffered and sacrificed without full understanding that My children and I are partners in the visible world.

I have decided that it is appropriate for Me to reveal the purpose of creation in year 2012. Henceforth My children can have deeper understanding when they choose to follow Me.

[Q] Thank you, God. May I ask how do we find you?

God : Many theologians and philosophers have provided reasons and arguments for My existence. These can provide useful perspectives. But mental concepts, mental reasoning and dualistic human language have their limits. I cannot be reasoned into existence. I cannot be rationalised into existence. I cannot be measured by your scientific instruments. I am divine Spirit. I am Cosmic Consciousness in the visible universe. I am the timeless Dimension. I am the divine Source who created the visible world.

My children need to know and understand that I am a Living God. I am living inside you in the form of spiritual essence, in the form of pure consciousness. The attributes of your spiritual essence or your soul are pure consciousness, moral consciousness and individualised cosmic energy, life force and intelligence.

To catch glimpses of My presence, please consider My ageless advice: "Be still and know that I am God." Your Western and Eastern wisdom teachers have conveyed to you that when you learn to meditate, when you experience tranquillity and mental stillness, your background silent awareness comes to the foreground. Slowly you catch glimpses of the 'silent witness' within. Your pure consciousness is a hologram of My cosmic consciousness. You can communicate with Me because your pure consciousness is conversing with Me. It is always connected to My cosmic consciousness. It is always connected to My love for you.

[Q] Thank you, God. May I ask: Why does the world exist? Why are there natural and moral evils?

God: These are deep issues for believers and non-believers. By emphasizing the occurrences of accidents, crimes, armed conflicts, wars, diseases, natural disasters and the abuse of free will, non-believers have sought to refute My presence. It is time for Me to explain these issues.

Let us begin from the beginning. Since eternity I have existed. I am the Source. I am the eternal One. I am all-knowing, all-good and all-powerful in the timeless Dimension.

First, My omniscience in the timeless Dimension is all-sufficient. I do not need to create a visible world to complement or prove My omniscience. If I wished to create a visible world so as to experience and enjoy it, I can create many types of visible worlds which are peaceful, beautiful and pleasant, without the occurrences of natural and moral evils, without the existence of human beings. This is congruent with My knowledge and wisdom. I do not need to create the type of visible world which human beings currently experience which is marked by existential uncertainty and suffering.

Second, My omnipotence in the timeless Dimension is all-sufficient. I do not need to create a visible world to complement or prove it. If I wished, I can create and eliminate visible worlds without human beings or creatures inhabiting them. If I wished, I can create beautiful and peaceful worlds so as to enjoy them, without the occurrences of natural and moral evils, without the existence of human beings. This is congruent with My power and wisdom.

Third, being all-good, I am Holiness. I am divine Goodness. But I am also divine Oneness. As divine Oneness in the timeless dimension, I do not have a physical body or bodies. I do not live in a space-time dimension. I am not individualized. I am not embodied.

In the timeless Dimension, it is natural that I do not have the opportunity to experience physical vulnerability and existential uncertainty. I do not have the opportunity to manifest dynamic moral goodness.

Dynamic moral goodness includes faith, humility, kindness, love, compassion, endurance and selfless service which humankind manifested when they performed compassionate deeds on earth. In addition, dynamic moral goodness requires Me to create individualized human beings or embodied souls. Dynamic moral goodness requires the interactions of individualised, embodied and vulnerable beings in a visible world. They need to experience trials and suffering to become mature. They need to exercise free will inherent in their waking consciousness to make moral decisions and perform good deeds. Thus, it is a natural condition of My divine Oneness that before the creation of the visible world and humankind, I have not yet manifested dynamic moral goodness.

For eternity, I have remained as divine Oneness. At some point during My eternity, I decided to create a visible world, so as to manifest dynamic moral goodness through My children. I decided that dynamic moral goodness in the visible world is a very valuable attribute which complements My attribute of divine Goodness in the timeless Dimension. I decided to create this stringent challenge for Me and for My children on earth.

Thus, I created this visible universe and humankind. I individualised My spiritual essence so as to live inside My children. My children and I are moral partners on earth. Through the pure consciousness of their souls, I share the life experiences of My children. Together we experience adversities, trials, and suffering. The purpose is for My children to become spiritually mature. As the voice of their souls, I encourage My children to do good. When the waking consciousness of My children chooses to listen to the voice of their souls, they become spiritually aware. They learn to walk the spiritual path.

When My children are honest, kind, sympathetic, faithful and compassionate in their daily lives, despite being physically vulnerable and facing existential uncertainty, they are manifesting dynamic moral goodness. When My children resolve to follow Me and choose to do good, despite trials and suffering, they are manifesting high-quality goodness. In these ways I manifest dynamic goodness through My children.

In human language, this can be called 'God is biting the bullet' theodicy. It means that I have decided that My divine Goodness in the timeless Dimension cannot forever remain untested and unproven. Therefore, during some point in eternity, I have decided to bite the bullet and create a stringent Self-challenge by providing freedom of choice to My children and by allowing the occurrences of natural and moral evils in a visible world. These give rise to existential uncertainty and suffering in the visible world. I have decided to experience and endure such existential uncertainty and suffering together with My children, so as to manifest dynamic moral goodness and contribute to the moral dimension of life.

In this way, My spiritually mature children are My moral partners. Guided by the voice of their souls, they strive and struggle in the visible world to manifest dynamic moral goodness under the stringent conditions of existential uncertainty and suffering. This attribute of dynamic moral goodness in the visible world complements My attribute of divine Goodness in the timeless dimension.

In the timeless Dimension, I am the Source. I am the eternal One. There is enduring peace, beauty, goodness and harmony in the timeless Dimension. I remain and continue to be all-knowing, all-good and all-powerful in the timeless Dimension.

In contrast, in the visible world, I have chosen to restrict My powers and omniscience. This arises from

My decision to bite the bullet and create a visible world which is subject to existential uncertainty and to the occurrences of natural and moral evils. Thus, I have chosen to limit My powers and omniscience in the visible world. I am no longer all-knowing and all-powerful in the visible world.

The visible world is a small part of the timeless Dimension. I created the laws of the natural sciences and mathematics when creating the visible world. Thereafter, I usually do not intervene directly in the visible world. This allows the occurrences of natural evils. The occurrences of natural evils introduce the crucial element of existential uncertainty into the visible world. They include earthquakes, hurricanes, floods, famines, accidents and diseases. These occur due to the operations of the laws of the sciences on earth.

I retain final control of the visible world. I can foresee the range of possible outcomes in the short term or longer term regarding an event or a cluster of events in the visible world. I can choose to occasionally intervene in an event or a cluster of events in the visible world. My decision to intervene is based on the range of possible outcomes of an event or a cluster of events and their long-term impact on the moral dimension of life. I have restricted My power of omniscience in the visible world. If I did not choose to intervene in an event or a cluster of events, I cannot foresee their actual final outcome in the visible world which is subject to the operations of the laws of the sciences and the free will of My children.

Another aspect is that I have restricted My omniscience and powers in the visible world by providing freedom of choice to My children. I do not intervene in the decisions and choices of My children. I also cannot foresee the final choice of My children regarding an event or a cluster of events facing them. I can only foresee the range of possible outcomes, based on the range of choices facing My children regarding an event or cluster of events. Once My child makes a decision and a choice and acts accordingly, I can better foresee the outcome of his choice.

I only intervene indirectly by encouraging My children to be conscientious and to do good through the voice of their souls. My children need to listen to the voice of their souls and choose to walk the path of righteousness. However, if some of My children decided to listen to their self-seeking desires and ignore the voice of their souls, they are walking the wrong path. They can commit deeds which harm others. Such moral evils give rise to another layer of existential uncertainty and suffering. On My part, through the voice of their souls, I continue to encourage the wrongdoers and the misguided to repent and urge them to walk the path of righteousness.

Once I decided to provide freedom of choice to My children, they need to decide and choose their daily conduct and deeds. I have decided to bite the bullet and I will not intervene in their choices. It is the will and resolve of My children to listen to the voice of their souls and walk the path of righteousness which enable My children and I to become partners on earth to manifest dynamic moral goodness and contribute to the moral dimension of life. In this way, we work towards fulfilling our crucial purpose on earth.

[Q] Thank you very much, God, for these revelations. May I enquire what are the necessary conditions for creating the dynamic moral dimension in the visible world?

God: The necessary conditions are:-

(1) I need to create a visible world and its laws. This is the visible universe with its many galaxies, stars and planets that are subject to the laws of mathematics and the laws of the sciences.

(2) In the visible universe, I am the Holy Spirit. I also manifest as Cosmic Consciousness and Cosmic Energy, Life Force and Intelligence.

(3) Regarding planet Earth, I created diverse life forms, including humankind. Human beings are My children and partners on earth. I have individualised My spiritual essence into souls which combine with their bodies when they are conceived.

(4) The embodied soul of My child will not remember its true identity when it is born in the visible world. This is to make the existential challenge authentic.

My children need to experience spiritual, mental and emotional growth during their journeys on earth so as to discover their real identity. They need to experience and endure physical vulnerability and existential uncertainty to become mature. Physical vulnerability means that My children experience the risks and dangers of harm or death arising from natural and moral evils. Existential uncertainty means that My children do not know what will happen to them the next moment as many external events are beyond their control. In addition, My children need to experience trials, suffering and adversities to become mature.

By not remembering their real identity when they are born, My children are also exposed to temptations due to selfish desires, lack of spiritual awareness and negative mental states. When I individualised into souls, the resultant souls are made aware of the challenges which they will be facing on earth as embodied souls. They have courageously accepted these challenges.

Every soul is also aware that if it cannot work in harmony with the body and its mental states, and the body committed harmful wrongdoing, the soul will need to undertake another or more human journeys on earth to contribute to human well-being. When it has sufficiently contributed to human well-being, the soul will return to My kingdom.

(5) The heart of the existential challenge for My children as embodied souls on earth is that their waking consciousness need to choose, under conditions of

physical vulnerability and existential uncertainty, whether to listen to the voice of the soul or to ignore it. This is the challenge of having free will or freedom of choice.

This choice has to be made by My children so as to manifest authentic goodness. The choice to become My instrument to do good has to be made by My children. I cannot choose for them. My children need to decide and choose.

Thus I created the conditions of physical vulnerability and existential uncertainty in the visible world so that My children will experience authentic moral challenge. My children will encounter situations where they need to consider which course of action is morally correct and which course of action is incorrect. They need to decide and choose how to act every day. Their decision and action will have moral significance for themselves and for other human beings.

(6) I created the possibilities for the occurrences of natural evil and moral evil in the visible world. First, natural evils such as earthquakes, floods, droughts and hurricanes occur due to the workings of natural laws on earth. The imprudent or irresponsible actions of human

beings in their industrialization programs can contribute to harmful climate changes. Second, moral evils arise from irresponsible or immoral deeds that harm others. These human beings are driven by strong self-seeking desires where their waking consciousness chooses not to listen to the voice of the soul.

The occurrences of natural and moral evils enable My children to cultivate valuable qualities in the longer term. These include faith, acceptance, endurance, humility, compassion, non-attachment and selfless service. In manifesting them, My children are making high-quality contributions to the moral dimension of life.

At the level of the visible world, natural and moral evils such as accidents, natural disasters, illnesses, physical disabilities, diseases and immoral deeds bring about the conditions of physical vulnerability and existential uncertainty. These are the risks and occurrences which My children need to endure and suffer, so as to make high-quality contributions to the moral dimension of life.

Please realise that when My children suffered due to natural and moral evils, I was suffering together with them. When My children endured and suffered undeserved pain, sorrow, afflictions and untimely deaths, I was suffering with them through their pure consciousness. As a responsible God, this is My decision. This is My choice. This is My commitment. My love for My children will never change. My love for My children is enduring.

(7) I retain ultimate long-term control of all events in the visible world. As the voice of their souls, I am intervening in the visible world by encouraging My children to be conscientious and to do good.

I will decide whether to intervene or not to intervene in the visible world regarding a specific event or a cluster of events. I will consider the long-term impact on the moral dimension of life when I am deciding the extent of My intervention. I retain the power to transform unfortunate events into long-term good.

(8) I created a visible world which is very real in the five-sensory sense. This is to make the existential challenge stringent and authentic. My children can be deceived into thinking that there is no eternal Dimension beyond the visible world. They need to study

and practise the perennial wisdom left by their spiritual ancestors to realise that there is an eternal Dimension.

The temptations and attractions of the visible world are conditions for seekers to experience another aspect of the dynamic moral challenge. They need to learn to overcome temptations. They need to cultivate prudence, honesty, self-restraint, self-discipline and non-attachment.

Further, there is no certainty of external success in the visible world. There is no certainty of external reward or recognition for performing good deeds. This enables My children to cultivate acceptance, humility, simplicity, non-attachment and submission to the guidance of the Holy Spirit.

To summarise, I created this visible world. It contains the necessary conditions for creating an authentic moral dimension. During their journeys on earth, I live inside the bodies of My children in the form of spiritual essence and pure consciousness. I experience their delight, excitement and joy as well as their pain, sorrow, suffering and physical deaths. If My children resolve to follow Me and become My instruments to do good, they have fulfilled their life purpose. It is the purity of My children's intention and commitment to perform a good deed with no expectation of return or recognition, or even at the expense of their well-being, which enhances the intrinsic value of the deed. This enhances the quality of their contribution to the moral dimension.

[Q] May I enquire: If human beings committed serious wrongdoing, what will happen to their souls?

God: Be assured that there is cosmic justice. Upon the death of the body, the disembodied soul will be assessed by My Holy Spirit. If this soul during its journey on earth had worked in harmony with the body and contributed to human well-being, it will be given a choice. It can choose to return to My kingdom of eternal harmony or begin another human journey on earth, so as to further contribute to the moral dimension of life.

If a soul during its journey on earth had endured undeserved suffering and untimely death, it can choose to return to My kingdom or begin another human journey, so as to contribute to the moral dimension of life.

If a soul during its journey on earth were not able to work in harmony with the body and its mental states, and the human body committed harmful wrongdoing due to selfish desires, upon the death of the body, My Holy Spirit will channel this soul to embark on one or more human journeys on earth. This is to enable this soul to contribute to human well-being. When it has sufficiently contributed to human well-being, it can return to My kingdom.

[Q] Why is the voice of the soul not able to guide us at all times to perform good deeds and prevent us from performing immoral deed?

God: It is a condition of the dynamic moral dimension that My children need to experience growth and development before they can become mature. Apart from learning to acquire practical knowledge and skills, they need to study and practise the perennial wisdom. Although they have moral consciousness, the self-seeking energies of some of My children are very strong. They can choose not to listen to the voice of their souls. They can perform selfish, immoral or criminal deeds under the erroneous thinking that these can enhance their well-being. This is due to a lack of spiritual awareness. They have not yet discovered their real identity.

In modern materialistic societies, as a child grows, its self-seeking energies tend to strengthen due to negative external conditioning. It can come from the family, friends, school and society which emphasise self-protection and self-advancement. The 'ego' starts to form due to self-seeking thoughts and thinking habits. The voice of the 'ego' will seek to crowd out the voice of the soul. Thus it is important to study and practise the perennial wisdom. My children can thereby understand the difference between 'healthy self-esteem' based on their real identity as children of God and 'unhealthy egoistic thoughts'. They can thereby learn to let go of selfish thoughts and motives.

[Q] May I enquire whether there are other purposes in creating this world?

God: The main life purpose of human beings is to contribute to the moral dimension. In the process of doing so, they can enjoy life and its many creative processes. They can enjoy music, literature, arts and the beauties of nature. They can pursue all kinds of socially acceptable activities and vocations to fulfil their potential based on their interests, abilities and talents. They should enjoy life in morally correct ways.

[Q] May I enquire if the main purpose of creation is to realise dynamic moral goodness, why are there so many different kinds of creatures and animals on earth?

God: Besides My main purpose, I created diversity to manifest My creative power.

[Q] In his best-selling series Conversations with God, Mr Neale Walsch wrote that Your purpose in creating the world is to experience it. How does this interpretation align with the above messages?

God: When Neale wrote his books, the time has not yet come for Me to reveal the ultimate purpose of creation. To experience the world through human beings is not My main purpose. To experience diversity in the visible world is secondary to My main purpose. My main purpose is to create an authentic moral dimension for My children and Me to manifest dynamic moral goodness.

Being omniscient and omnipotent, I could have created a material visible world with no human beings and with no animal or insect life on a peaceful planet. I could create only plant life and beautiful rivers, meadows, hills, lakes, mountains, seas and oceans. I could choose to manifest Myself in the visible world as Cosmic Consciousness to enjoy experiences in the visible world. This will avoid the enormous amount of pain and suffering experienced by many generations of humankind and by Me on earth due to natural and moral evils.

I could also create compassionate, pure-hearted angelic beings with perceptive, sensory and reflective abilities. They would always choose to do good. I could endow them with invulnerable spiritual bodies that do not get hurt, do not fall sick and do not die. These pure-hearted, immortal angelic beings can inhabit My aforesaid visible world. I could also impose a limited lifespan on these angelic beings. Thereafter I could choose to individualise My Cosmic Consciousness and live within the spiritual bodies of these angelic beings as their pure consciousness. I can thereby experience the visible world through their eyes and senses. This will avoid the enormous amount of pain and suffering experienced by many generations of humankind and by Me on earth due to natural and moral evils.

There are many permutations whereby I might have created peaceful and beautiful visible worlds which are congruent with My knowledge, wisdom and power, which I can enjoy and experience, without the occurrences of natural and moral evils, without existential suffering.

I am not a sadistic God. I am not a malevolent God. Why would I want to create stringent conditions in a visible world with occurrences of natural and moral evils which will cause enormous pain and suffering to Me and My children. My ultimate purpose is to attain a Greater Good which is to manifest dynamic moral goodness.

[Q] Thank you, God. May I ask the extent of your intervention in the visible world. For example, some months ago I read a newspaper report where a five-year-old child was killed in a car accident. Recently there was the tragic shooting incident at Connecticut in the United States where twenty children were killed by a mentally

disturbed person. I also learnt about the death of hundreds of children during the year 2008 earthquake in China. I was very sad to learn about these events. Please enlighten me.

God: I understand your sadness. I understand your confusion. It is also very sad for Me. Please be assured that I lived in all of these children in the form of spiritual essence and pure consciousness. I was living inside them. I experienced their ordeals together with them. I was with them until their last moment. I provided them with strength. I suffered their trials, pain and deaths. Their eternal life in My kingdom is assured. I also experienced the anguish, pain and grief of their parents, relatives and friends. "Blessed are those who mourn ..."

Please be assured that the souls of these children have since returned to My kingdom of eternal joy and harmony. They have also been given the choice either to permanently return to My kingdom or to return to earth for another human journey.

May I provide further insights. In the case of the five-year-old child who was killed in the car accident, her death enabled the driver to learn a deep lesson. In addition, many other drivers have been reminded by this accident to be very careful. From this larger perspective, many other children and adults need not be harmed and they need not die. Thus, the death of that child has saved the lives of many other children and adults.

Regarding the tragic Connecticut shooting where twenty children were killed, this tragedy will lead the authorities to tighten laws on gun sales and purchase. In the longer term, this will reduce such violence, resulting in the saving of many lives.

Regarding the earthquake, this is a large-scale tragedy. The earthquake occurred due to natural geological laws. I intervened to reduce the number of injuries and deaths. Please be assured that the moral and spiritual qualities manifested by the parents, relatives and friends of the victims in terms of compassion, love, courage and the determination to move on with life exceeded the suffering due to injuries and deaths. Their contributions to the dynamic moral dimension of life are enormous.

Please remember that in every large-scale tragedy including floods, epidemics, armed conflicts and wars, I lived inside each of the victims, casualties, patriots and defenders of freedom and human rights. I experienced, endured and suffered their trials, pain and afflictions. I was with each of them until their last breath, until their last moment. They have since returned to My kingdom or they have chosen to experience another human journey on earth.

[Q] Thank you, God. Why did you not create a visible world with no undeserved suffering and no untimely death, with no crimes and no moral evil?

God : I could have created a crime-free world. I could have created a world with no moral evil. I could have created a world with no abuse of free will. But this means that there is no genuine free will. There is no genuine freedom of choice. It is limited free will, subject to My intervention which prevents a human being from committing a wrongdoing. This will not enable the emergence of an authentic moral dimension in the visible world. My original purpose will fail. My decision to create a stringent challenge for Me and for My children on earth will fail.

I could have remained as divine Goodness at the level of the timeless Dimension. I need not choose to manifest dynamic moral goodness through My children on earth. But once I made the decision to create a stringent challenge so as to manifest authentic moral goodness in a visible world, the natural consequences need to follow. The conditions for an authentic moral dimension in a visible world need to be created. I have explained these conditions earlier.

[Q] Please enlighten me: why did You create the 'dynamic' moral dimension when You foresee and know that this entails enormous suffering due to the occurrences of natural and moral evils?

God: For eternity I have existed as Holiness and divine Goodness at the level of the timeless Dimension. At some point during My eternity, I made the crucial decision to create a visible world. This is to enable My children to manifest dynamic moral goodness. This is to enable Me to contribute to such manifestation. It is a stringent challenge for Me and for My children on earth.

I have decided that as divine Goodness, I cannot forever remain untested and unproven at the level of the visible world with its characteristics of physical vulnerability, existential uncertainty, pain, suffering and death. I need to experience these suffering and afflictions through My children, so as to contribute to manifesting dynamic moral goodness through My children. This attribute of dynamic moral goodness in the visible world will complement My attribute of divine Goodness at the level of the timeless Dimension. I have decided that dynamic moral goodness in the visible world is a highly valuable attribute. It is My decision. It is My choice. It is My commitment.

Thus, in human language, I need to bite the bullet. This emphasizes My decision, My choice and My commitment to experience, suffer and endure this stringent challenge which I have created for Myself and for My children on earth. The main thrust of this challenge is to manifest authentic moral goodness in the visible world under the conditions of physical vulnerability and existential uncertainty.

One astonishing revelation to you is that from the perspective of the timeless Dimension, when I am perceiving your visible world as the divine Source, your visible world is over for Me. From the timeless Dimension, billions of years at the level of the visible universe are a short span of time for Me. The visible universe reflects a small part of My Power and Strength.

If you have a pair of eyes as large as ten galaxies, you will observe that the daily rotations of the earth and its revolutions around the Sun will be very fast. Thus, as My timeless Dimension is many times larger than your visible universe, I am like having a tremendously large pair of eyes observing the rapid birth, growth and evolution of this visible universe until it no longer can support morally conscious life. As I am communicating with you now, it is over for Me at the level of the timeless Dimension. I have completed My experiences of the dynamic moral dimension in the visible world. Together with My children we have manifested dynamic moral goodness. At the level of the timeless Dimension, My children on earth are living in My cosmic past.

From year 2013 onwards, based on these revelations, My children will have deeper understanding of the ultimate purpose of creation. They can more confidently choose to follow Me, to do good and to contribute to the moral dimension of life.

On My part, I continue to live inside My children in the form of spiritual essence and pure consciousness.

This will never change. My love for My children on earth remains the same. As the voice of their souls, I will continue to encourage My children to be conscientious and to do good. I will continue to experience what they experience in the visible world. My love for My children on earth is eternal. When their journeys on earth end, their souls will sooner or later return to My kingdom.

[Q] Thank you very much, God. Before we end our dialogue, may I enquire whether You have precepts for us to follow?

God: I have distilled Four Wisdom Principles. Please practise them daily.

First Wisdom Principle:
Please discover the unconditional love of God.

Be still and know that I am God. Be still and discover My unconditional love for you. To discover My unconditional love for you, please release self-seeking thoughts and desires. Replace them with compassionate thoughts to assist the needy. You can expand your spiritual awareness by listening to inspiring music, reading the Psalms, reading a devotional book, appreciating works of art, walking at the seaside, meditating or contemplating. These activities can soften self-seeking energies. They help to loosen your mental attachments to external success.

Please allocate 'spiritual workout time' every day to engage in some of these activities. Please learn to meditate and touch the silence within. Gradually you will reach a state with minimal thoughts and few desires. You begin to catch glimpses of the freedom and joy of not being driven by self-seeking energies. You learn to release your consciousness from the trap of self-seeking thoughts.

If you learn to meditate, by letting of thoughts, feelings and desires, the background of 'silent' consciousness comes naturally to the foreground. You catch glimpses of the 'pure consciousness' within. Gradually you realise that this is an attribute of your soul or spiritual essence. This is an attribute of My presence. This is My individualised cosmic consciousness. You catch glimpses of the truth that I am always with you, that you are always connected to My love. You catch glimpses of your soul which is always wholesome, pure and intact. Your soul will return to My kingdom when your journey on earth ends. These are My priceless gifts to you. These gifts are always within you.

Based on this realization, please engage in spiritual workout activities. Continue to meditate and touch the silence within. The more often you glimpse My priceless gifts within you, the lesser is your attachment to worldly success. Spiritual contentment, inner peace and gratefulness emerge. You experience contentment by glimpsing the truths that you are always sustained by My love, wisdom, compassion and peace. What everyone is looking for is inner peace. What you truly need are My love and inner peace. By glimpsing My priceless gifts, you realise that I have given you inner peace. You are always connected to My love. My gifts are more than sufficient for all your needs.

My unconditional love does not require you to become perfect. It does not require you to surpass others. It does not require you to become famous, wealthy or powerful. It does not require you to struggle for external success or first-rate performance. The foundational principle is that you listen to your conscience and make a commitment to follow Me day by day, holding onto the belief that I am divine Truth and Goodness.

By glimpsing these unchanging truths, when you encounter setbacks, you learn to rely on My strength. Slowly you learn to release your feelings of fear, anxiety and confusion. You realise that these feelings are temporary. They are flashes of mental energy that arise and pass away. Only your essence is real and eternal. Only My love for you is real and eternal.

Above all, by glimpsing My love for you and My priceless gifts within you, you realise the importance of listening to your conscience, the voice of your soul. Slowly you realise the importance of choosing to be responsible to Me day by day. In this way you affirm that you are "a child of God". You affirm that "Every day is a bonus to do something beautiful for God".

Every day is a precious gift from Me. It is a precious gift for you to grow spiritually. It is a precious gift for you to deepen awareness of your real identity. It is a precious gift for you to extend a kind thought, word or deed to others. You may also wish to imagine that you have passed away yesterday. In this way you can more deeply appreciate the preciousness of a new day.

You become more attentive to how you spend your time daily, how you show thankfulness to those who have helped you. You learn to reassess your values and daily commitments. You become less attached to external success. You become attentive to the nature of your daily wishes, whether they are in harmony with the voice of your soul.

Second Wisdom Principle: Please remain humble, attentive, compassionate and forgiving.

Please remain humble, attentive and vigilant at all times regarding the nature of your thoughts, feelings and desires. As long as you are in the flesh, you cannot outgrow temptations.

You will continue to experience unhealthy thoughts and desires. They can arise due to pride, greed, anger, jealousy and desire for sensual pleasure. If your spiritual maturity is high, you experience them less. If you are spiritually less mature, you experience them more often. Thus, please maintain your humility and vigilance. Avoid activities that reinforce unhealthy thoughts and desires.

When temptations arise in your mind, please repeat the words "Peace of God" or "Love of God" or "Power of God". You can repeat appropriate substitutes that can effectively calm your mind. Please repeat them until your waking consciousness is calmed, until it is no longer driven by unhealthy thoughts. Please repeat them until you are aware that you are always connected to My love.

Further, please listen to the kind intentions of your soul. Choose to be sympathetic, compassionate and forgiving. Choose to forgive by realising that people behave according to their level of spiritual and moral awareness. Deepen your trust in God's timing for the spiritual growth of the people you interact in your lives.

When you forgive the selfish words or deeds of others, you are letting go of resentment or hatred. You realise that the selfish deeds of others arose due to their inner afflictions. They have not yet discovered their real identity. They have not yet discovered inner peace. They performed selfish deeds under the misconception that such deeds would provide them with security and happiness. They performed selfish deeds under the misconception that such deeds would protect their pride, appease their anger or lessen their envy.

Thus, inwardly, you learn to forgive them. You learn to forgive their moments of spiritual non-awareness. Pray that they will awaken soon. Outwardly you continue to voice your objections to selfish, immoral and criminal deeds. You focus your objections on the deeds and not on the persons.

Further, if you slip into spiritual non-awareness and perform a selfish or immoral deed, do repent sincerely and seek My forgiveness. Please find appropriate ways to make amends and recommit yourself to follow Me and walk the spiritual path. Every day affirm your commitment to live a life of honesty, kindness and compassion.

Third Wisdom Principle:
Please remain faithful to God day by day.

Regardless of external events, regardless of your doubts and fear, please follow Me and remain faithful to Me. This is the best manifestation of your love for Me.

As an embodied and vulnerable human being, your waking consciousness will experience periodic doubts and uncertainty about My wisdom, goodness and power. Slowly learn to let go of and rise above these mental doubts and fear. They are temporary. They are only flashes of mental energies. They arise and pass away. Only your spiritual essence is real.

Please make a commitment each day to endure unfortunate events that occur to you. Quietly sustain your faith in Me. Pray to Me for strength. Choose to believe that what I decide for you is for your eternal good, for your eternal best. Remind yourself that your finite mind may not be able to see how I will transform unfortunate events into long-term good.

Fourth Wisdom Principle:
Please serve God's purposes day by day.

You serve My purposes by learning to replace negative thoughts with positive thoughts day by day.

Please remember that sincere efforts in doing good reflect inner success. There is no failure when doing good.

If you are physically and mentally healthy, you will become a care-giver. Please use your practical skills and knowledge, and extend helping hands to those who need your care and assistance. If you are physically unwell and become a care-receiver, please realise that you are also contributing to the moral dimension of life. You are manifesting faith and trust in Me. You are manifesting patience, humility and wisdom in relying on Me, in continuing to love Me, despite your suffering. Your faith can inspire others. You are also providing opportunities to others for them to develop and deepen their compassion.

Please develop your spiritual strength and cheerfulness by replacing negative thoughts with positive thoughts. You can do so by reading the following affirmations every day:

"Regardless of external events, I choose to remain faithful to God every day. I choose to be honest, kind and helpful every day. I choose to replace negative thoughts with positive thoughts every day. By performing little acts of kindness, I choose to do something beautiful for God day by day.

I am a spiritual being. I am a child of God. This is my real identity. My spiritual essence or my soul is always wholesome, pure and intact. It is timeless. It is indestructible. No people and no events can affect it. Nothing can impair it. My soul comes from God. My soul will return to the kingdom of God when my journey on earth ends.

With the blessings of God, every day is a bonus. Every day is a bonus to receive and to share. Every day is a bonus to receive the priceless gifts of God -- His gifts of love, wisdom, compassion, strength, peace and hope. May I learn to share these gifts with others. May I choose to regard every day as a bonus to share the best within me. May I learn and keep learning practical skills and knowledge, so that I can effectively assist others to enhance their well-being.

With the help of God, I can do all positive things. With the guidance of the Holy Spirit, I can do all positive things. Thus, I choose to serve others, to extend help and assistance to the needy. In this way I am contributing to the moral dimension of life. In this way I am fulfilling my life's purpose.

With the guidance of the Holy Spirit, may I realise that self-seeking thoughts, feelings and desires are only flashes of mental energies. They are temporary. They are not solid entities. I can learn to meditate and watch them arise and pass away against the background of 'pure consciousness'. I can choose positive and healthy thoughts. I can become a positive and helpful person.

With the blessings of God, regardless of external success, I have not lived in vain. By living one day at a time, by living one moment at a time, by being considerate and helpful to others, I have attained inner success. By listening to my conscience, I have attained inner success. By making a commitment to follow God day by day, I have attained inner success. I may be a nobody in the eyes of the world. But I am always Somebody in the eyes of God. I am always a precious child of God. If I made mistakes or committed a wrongdoing, I will repent, seek God's forgiveness, find appropriate ways to make amends and move on with life.

May I realise that God cares for my eternal best. Whatever God decides for me, it is for my eternal good.

God is with me and inside me all the time, enjoying life experiences together with me, encouraging me and suffering the bad times together with me. God always cares for my eternal best.

May I realise that God is my genuine long-term Employer. I am never unemployed. Spiritually I am never out of work. As long as I am conscientious and helpful every day, as long as I extend a kind word or deed to others, I have done good for the day. I have done something beautiful for God.

May I learn to live as if I had died yesterday, so that each day is a bonus to follow God, to become His instrument to do good. May I learn to live as if I had died yesterday, so that each day is a bonus to receive the priceless gifts of God and to share them with others. When God decides to bring me home, my soul will return to His kingdom, to eternal peace and harmony. I am very grateful to God for His eternal love."

Merton Lee: Thank you, God, for these revelations and messages. Thank you very much.

***

Notes

A Spring of Hope

[1] This is an original article written by the author. It is inspired by an article from pages 28 to 29 of the book *Glad To Be Me* by Pereta Elkins (Prentice-Hall, 1976).

[2] "Wisdom" is an original story written by the author. "A new prayer from Jesus" is an original article

written by the author. The prayers of Saint Teresa of Avila and Saint Francis are based on the Wikipedia articles on Saint Teresa and Saint Francis.

[3] This true story is an abridged version based on the Wikipedia article on pastor Russell Conwell.

[4] This story is a summarized version of the children's story *The Giving Tree* by Shel Silverstein (Harper and Row, 1964).

[5] This true story is abridged from the Wikipedia articles on Anne Sullivan and Helen Keller.

[6] "When Pebbles Share The Mystery" is a poem written by the author.

A Summer of Strength

[1] This story is revised and written by the author, based on a traditional Eastern tale.

[2] This true story is based on the Wikipedia article on Buckminster Fuller.

[3] This true story is based on internet articles on the biography of Annie Johnson Flint.

[4] This true story is based on the Wikipedia article on Edwarda O'Bara.

[5] "Honored in Heaven" is an original story written by the author.

[6] "Miraculous Joe" is an abridged version of a true story in Dr Gerald Jampolsky's book *Love Is Letting Go of Fear* (Celestial Arts, 1979).

[7] "Miraculous Minister of Hope" is based on Don Piper's book *Daily Devotions Inspired by 90 Minutes in Heaven* (Berkley Publishing Group, 2006).

[8] "Miraculous Faith" is a true story abridged from Max Lucado's book *It's Not About Me* (Integrity Publishers, 2004).

[9] "Miraculous Nick Vujicic" is a true story abridged from Nick's book *Life Without Limits* (Doubleday, 2010).

[10] "Miraculous Saint Maximilian Kolbe" is abridged from the Wikipedia article on Saint Maximilian Kolbe.

An Autumn of Faith

[1] "The Twins" is written by the author. It is inspired by a story told by Dr Wayne Dyer in *Your Sacred Self* (Harper Collins, 1995).

[2] "Pointing To The Truth" is written by the author. It is inspired by a traditional Eastern tale.

[3] "The Four Rivers" is an original story written by the author.

[4] "Is it day time or night time?" is revised and rewritten by the author. It is inspired by a traditional wisdom tale.

[5] “Those Daily Seasons” is a poem written by the author.

21835431R00108

Printed in Great Britain
by Amazon